Leading
In Public Prayer

Leading
In Public Prayer

Andrew W. Blackwood

ABINGDON PRESS
NEW YORK • NASHVILLE

LEADING IN PUBLIC PRAYER

Copyright © MCMLVIII by Abingdon Press

Library of Congress Catalog Card Number: 58-7429

SET UP, PRINTED, AND BOUND BY THE
PARTHENON PRESS, AT NASHVILLE,
TENNESSEE, UNITED STATES OF AMERICA

DEDICATED

to the Minister

Who Gets People to Pray in Church

Foreword

THIS BOOK AIMS TO HELP A LOCAL PASTOR OR A SEMINARY
student with the most difficult part of the ministry today.
Sooner or later every parish minister becomes concerned about
his public prayers. Without knowing the history of worship
a person may experiment, as I used to do, with a resulting
sense of futility. If a son of the parsonage enlists for the ministry, the father hopes that in the seminary the young man
will learn what lies back of the prayers in church. By way of
encouraging such a father or his son, I am opening up my
heart to tell what I have learned, first by trial and error, and
later by conferring with others and by reading books.

As a boy I grew up among church folk who stressed everything about the sermon, but cared little about the form of
public prayers. Later at two university chapels I learned to
admire, and in the right sense to enjoy, prayers almost as
beautiful as the music. I saw that the "beauty of holiness"
could find a voice in prayers as well as in songs. During
seventeen years in the pastorate my prayers in church fell far
short of the ideal, but now I look back on that leadership
with thanksgiving for the opportunity and with longing that
it were mine once again.

At Princeton Seminary every year for two decades I taught a
course in public worship, with stress on the prayers. Soon I
discovered that I needed to know the history, starting with the

Old Testament and giving priority to the New. So I traced the development, and the later decline, of public prayer. I also welcomed every opportunity to take part in various forms of Christian worship.

Gradually I worked out the practical philosophy that undergirds this book. If I fail to give any person credit, I can only plead that I have lived so much with the writings of Friedrich Heiler, Evelyn Underhill, and others that an adopted brain child may seem my very own. Really, "I have nothing that I have not received," mainly from the Holy Scriptures. I look on the Bible as the inspired source book of Christian worship, and as the authoritative guidebook in public prayer.

No writer or professor can tell anyone else how to lead in public prayer. In this loftiest of holy arts everyone called of God must "work out [his] own salvation with fear and trembling" (Phil. 2:12). There can be no binding rules, save the injunction to follow the guidance of the Holy Spirit, and to toil in preparing "beaten oil for the sanctuary." Hence the fathers used to tell us: "Pray because everything depends on God, and work as though everything depended on you."

This book does not consist of "easy lessons about leading in public prayer." Such leadership calls for vastly more than a mellifluous voice and a mastery of musical words. As C. H. Spurgeon once said, the man who guides others into the presence of the King must have journeyed far into the King's country, and often have looked upon His face. In the light of such experiences, day after day, the man honored of God as a leader in public prayer learns to speak for others in ways distinctly his own. Herein lies the secret of growth in effectiveness, in power, and in joy.

ANDREW WATTERSON BLACKWOOD

Contents

PART TWO

The Preparation for Leading

PART ONE

The Prayers
in Public Worship

CHAPTER I

Looking at
Our Public Prayers

PRAYER HAS ALWAYS FORMED A MOST IMPORTANT PART OF Christian worship. Worship here means God's way of revealing Himself to His children in church, and their ways of responding to Him in faith. Without pausing to consider private devotions, or the family altar, we are to deal only with prayers in corporate worship. In God's revelation of Himself, the reading of the Scriptures and the preaching of the Gospel form all-important parts. In the responses from the people, prayers and praises likewise form all-important parts. In the sacraments, or ordinances, Baptism and the Lord's Supper, the elements of revelation and response both appear, with still more of mystery.

Opinions differ about the relative importance of various parts in public worship. Without entering into an argument about the respective merits of prayer, praise, and preaching, let us take for granted that the entire hour of worship is more important than any component part. Let us also assume that no one can overestimate the importance of the public prayers. What then should they mean to the person who leads in worship and to the people who join in public prayer, whether audibly or silently? Still more vital, what do they mean to the

15

One whom we worship? Before we formulate replies to these difficult questions, we should think about the setting of the prayers in the public worship of God.

A Rediscovery of Public Worship

Our century has witnessed a widespread renewal of concern about public worship. Here in the States, as in Great Britain and on the Continent, almost every branch of the Christian Church has been showing increased concern about the meaning and the practice of corporate worship. Bodies with prescribed forms, both Protestant and Roman Catholic, have encouraged scholarly research into the origins and the development of public worship. Nonliturgical groups, such as the Friends, have striven to make uncharted ways in church worship still more worthy of their traditions and ideals.

More than a few denominations stand somewhere between liturgical and nonliturgical bodies. For convenience we shall refer to this "in-between" attitude under the heading of "free worship." All these labels are loose. How can we mortals employ accurate terms in discussing the mystery of public worship? Again, for convenience, we shall think of free worship as permitting the local church and its minister to use historic forms of worship, or to dispense with such use. Among major denominations with free worship the trend of late has been distinctly toward larger use of historic forms.

This label, free worship, like the others, has limitations. To the unschooled it may even suggest that Scotsmen believe in worship "without money and without price." In no case ought the use of such a term to suggest either boasting or stigma. All we Protestants doubtless feel sure that our particular ways of worship accord with the ideals of the New Testament. We who believe in free worship ought gladly to

16

acknowledge that in the history of the Church to this hour the Lord has repeatedly blessed ways of public worship far different from our own. "Where the Spirit of the Lord is, there is liberty." (II Cor. 3:17b.) Even in New Testament times, according to B. H. Streeter and other Bible scholars, different congregations worshiped in various ways. Instead of quarreling about variety in form, let us thank God that He stands ready to bless all who "worship [Him] in spirit and in truth."

Increased Concern About Public Prayers

The renewal of concern about public worship has drawn attention especially to the prayers. Fifty years ago a foremost divinity school could escape criticism while devoting practically no attention to the training of young men for leading in public prayer. Except among Lutherans and Episcopalians, only an occasional seminary emphasized any part of public worship other than the reading of the Scriptures and the preparation of sermons. Partly for this reason, many of us went into the active ministry unaware of the difficulty in preparing to lead a corporate prayer. More than a few of us who preached acceptably did not make ready for leading in prayer.

Later many young pastors began to read books about public worship. They also learned much by joining in prayer with leader after leader who took time to make ready for speaking to God on behalf of a waiting throng. Many a young minister began to tinker with the order of worship, as though anyone could devise a helpful succession of sickly devotions. Still others began to experiment with patchwork prayers, which tried to combine the simplicity of childlike devotions with

17

O Thou by whom we come to God—
The Life, the Truth, the Way!
The path of prayer Thyself hast trod;
Lord, teach us how to pray! [2]

The history of worship shows that often it has proved hard to keep emotion in its proper place, not least in public prayer. With nothing but the expression of feelings, unrestrained public worship, so-called, may become as non-Christian as a snake dance among Hopi braves. Without any expression of feeling, a so-called public prayer may be no more spiritual than the snow on "Greenland's icy mountains." In such an earnest effort, devoid of emotion, the pastor may merely "get across to the people" something he thinks they ought to know or do.

Any such leader ought to study *A Treatise Concerning Religious Affections* (1746) by Jonathan Edwards. That mighty philosopher pleaded for the Christian primacy of the feelings, though never apart from the governance of a disciplined will. In the light of God's revealed truth, under the guidance of the Holy Spirit, a leader in public prayer ought to have a heart full of sacred fire that refuses to stay hidden. In the House of Prayer this living flame ought to set other hearts afire for God.

In the study on Saturday morning how can an educated minister feel sure that on the morrow his prayers will cause the hearts of God's children to burn and their faces to glow with light from above? On the basis of God's revealed truth, how can he feel sure of voicing their desires and aspirations, instead of merely communicating religious ideas and practical suggestions? Alas, no one can put into words the "tone

[2] James Montgomery, "What Is Prayer?"

color" of a public prayer, as distinct from that of an intelligent sermon. Even so, a finding from another field may help a pastor to sense the difference. According to psychology, when a speaker's emotions are strongly moved, his words flow in what has become known as prose rhythm.[3] Conversely, if in vocal prayer a man's words do not flow, at least gently, he may not be praying.

Two examples from masters of writing may show the difference between words that teach Christian truth and others that voice Christian feeling. According to Friedrich Heiler, "Public worship has [always] been the native home of Christian faith and life." What an intelligent statement of fact, and how remote from the spirit of prayer! On the other hand, think of words suitable for use at vespers, and at other times of worship. Note how John Henry Newman expresses emotion under the guidance of a disciplined will, and how the words flow with the gentle movement of prose full of feeling:

O Lord, support us all the day long of this troublous life, until the shadows lengthen and the evening comes, and the busy world is hushed, and the fever of life is over, and our work is done. Then of Thy mercy grant us a safe lodging, and a holy rest, and peace at the last; through Jesus Christ our Lord. Amen.

If a pastor wishes to know whether or not his public prayers express feeling, he may try a simple experiment. Through a lay friend the minister can arrange for a tape or a disk recording of all that he says during a morning hour of worship. The next day, alone with his Lord, he can listen to what he has said, both Godward in the prayers and manward in the ser-

[3] See George Saintsbury, A History of English Prose Rhythm (London: Macmillan & Co., Ltd., 1912).

mon. Without being able to analyze all the facts in the case, he ought to find that he speaks to the heavenly Father in a way unlike that in which he addresses men. He employs a different sort of semi-rhythmical speech, though never with singsong, which cannot be Christian, because it is not intelligent. Singsong may put saints to sleep. If yesterday he led others in prayer and did not merely voice religious ideas, on Monday his words ought to flow, and once more his heart ought to feel strangely moved.

The man who excels in pastoral visitation and counseling ought to excel in public prayer. He has a heart. On the contrary, a pulpit master may not know people, or care to know them. By "eloquent prayers," which call attention to themselves, he may delight persons who never have had to suffer, but how can he voice the desires of a young wife who has bidden farewell to her first-born babe, and learns that she will never have another? Both in prayer, and in preaching, the "all-round minister," or "pastoral director," [4] meets the needs of churchgoers whom he knows and loves. When he speaks to God in prayer, he causes lovers of the Bible to feel that angels of God are ascending with the desires of His children. When the minister preaches, spiritual-minded hearers feel that angels are descending with tidings of mercy from the God who cares about all the needs and desires of His children.

Loving Sacrifices to God

Looking beneath the expression of feeling, let us think of public prayer in terms of loving sacrifice to God. According to the *Shorter Catechism*, "Prayer is an offering up." This means sacrifice, or oblation. The latter term is the more accurate, as

[4] See the able book by H. Richard Niebuhr, *The Purpose of the Church and Its Ministry* (New York: Harper & Bros., 1956).

it usually refers to giving the Lord something without life. Strictly speaking, Christ offered Himself on Golgotha as a sacrifice for our sins; in prayer we bring to God our oblations. The two terms, "sacrifice" and "oblation," are often employed interchangeably. Whatever the terminology, there can be no doubt that according to the New Testament our prayers and praises ought to take the place of Hebrew sacrifices. Naturally there must be differences, for the New Testament puts public worship on a loftier plane than does the Old.

Our public prayers should do today what Hebrew sacrifices did in other times.[5] At least ideally, they embodied the responses of the people to God's revelation of Himself. According to Isaiah and other prophetic interpreters, the value of those sacrifices depended largely on the motives of the worshipers. Isaiah could never forget that his own transforming vision of God and duty had come in terms of sacrificial worship (6:1-8). Throughout their public ministry, he and other seers, notably Amos, gave the people no rest until their offerings in worship represented the dominant feelings of their hearts.

Today we largely ignore this element of sacrifice in prayer. We rejoice to believe that through His once offering Himself up as a sacrifice for "us men and for our salvation," Christ set us free from sin, and from the Hebrew sacrificial system. Sometimes we assail Romanists for seeming to perpetuate those "outmoded rites." Should we not, as Protestants, search our own hearts and our ways of worship to make sure that we have carried out the New Testament teachings about prayer

[5] Books of reference include George B. Gray, *Sacrifice in the Old Testament* (London: Oxford University Press, 1925); W. O. E. Oesterley, *The Jewish Background of the Christian Liturgy* (London: Oxford University Press, 1925).

23

and praise as sacrifices to God? Especially should the minister look upon himself as appointed to lead in offering oblations of prayer. Whether or not he refers to his ministry as priestly, any pastor can learn much about public prayer by making a careful study of the Hebrew sacrifices (Lev. 1–7).

A man set apart and trained to lead in public worship ought to take all these duties seriously. Like a worthy priest of old, a pastor should mingle with his people as their "friend, counselor, and guide," sent from God. At stated times of worship he should lead them in prayer: that is, in offering up loving sacrifices. As a motto to hang in the study he may adopt the words of King David, words that show a commendable attitude toward public worship: "I cannot offer burnt-offerings to the Lord my God that cost me nothing" (II Sam. 24:24 Amer. Trans.).

Everything so far points to one conclusion: before a minister dares to lead in public prayer, he ought to make ready as carefully as time and opportunity permit. In case of an emergency he may have to lead without time to prepare, but after long years in the ministry few of us can recall many such occasions. When a man of God controls his use of time, and makes his own weekly schedule, he should give priority to what matters most: his preparation to pray and to preach. Such preparation includes being a faithful pastor and counselor. Next to God, nothing else in the ministry matters so much as being a good man, a good pastor, a good leader in prayer, and a good preacher. These all belong together. This practical philosophy appears in an article by Nathaniel Micklem, who makes a strong case for free worship. Here he writes about "Ex Tempore Prayer":

24

Ex tempore prayer is not to be identified with unpremeditated prayer. I have never understood why the holy Spirit should require a minister to prepare the words of his sermon in his study and should disapprove of the preparation of his prayers.

No minister should be tied to the words of his sermon-manu-script nor to the words of his own or another man's written prayers. But where a Free Church minister knows the rich field of liturgical tradition and is free and wise to use, to adapt, to apply it for the worship of his congregation, he has an incomparable advantage over the parson who is largely bound by Matins and by Evensong.[6]

A young reader may ask: "How can I spare all the time it will take to make ready for public prayer every week, and gradually learn all that I need to know about this difficult sub-ject?" A veteran replies, most humbly: "My friend, how can you invest a major portion of God's time more profitably and more happily than by living with people, so as to sense their heart needs, and by living near to God, so as to lead your friends to 'the Father of mercies, and the God of all com-fort' (II Cor. 1:3b)? Every week make ready for public prayer as well as you will wish to have done when you are seventy years of age."

> Youth shows but half; trust God:
> See all, nor be afraid! [7]

---

[6] *The British Weekly*, October 10, 1957, p. 4. Used by permission of author and publisher.

[7] Robert Browning, "Rabbi Ben Ezra."

CHAPTER II

Following a General Pattern

IN AN HOUR OF PUBLIC WORSHIP THE PRAYERS OUGHT TO FORM integral parts of an organic whole. According to Paul, "All things should be done decently and in order" (I Cor. 14:40 R.S.V.) As Moffatt translates the word, "decently" means "decorously." In other words, at church be a "gentleman toward God." Plan for prayers in keeping with the character of the One whom Christians worship. The Lord does everything according to a plan of His own making. Often He works so silently and inconspicuously that His undergirding plan calls no attention to itself. The Holy Spirit stands ready to guide every pastor in discovering and following the best pattern for any hour of worship, with special reference to the prayers.

A Legacy from the Past

When Paul wrote about doing all such things "decently and in order," he may have been thinking about his boyhood experiences in a synagogue at Tarsus. As every reader knows, the stated hour of worship in a synagogue proceeded in an orderly fashion, with special emphasis on the prayers. Later when the Apostle wrote to a "young church" in a Grecian city, he called for much the same sort of propriety and reverence. In like manner, every leader of public prayer today should feel that he is "the heir of all the ages." For the entire heritage of worship he should often give thanks to God.

At present we cannot make even a hasty survey of public worship in history, starting with Old Testament times.[1] After the days of the apostles various streams flowed together so that throughout Europe prior to the Reformation there was formed a mighty stream of would-be devotion. Since the days of Luther and Calvin all sorts of ways in church have abounded. In almost all the Protestant churches a student can find various attitudes toward public prayer. These differences a seminary professor senses when he goes about among congregations with practically the same doctrinal beliefs, but with little uniformity in ways of prayer. At present we are to think about such things in a congregation neither strongly liturgical nor aggressively antiliturgical.

Among "in-between churches" there is a sort of underlying unity in ways of prayer. In almost every service that follows a basic plan, five elements appear in the prayers, often in the same order. This order appears in a homely acrostic, ACTSS. By doubling the final consonant in the name of a major New Testament book, the acrostic calls for Adoration—Confession—Thanksgiving—Supplication (including both Petitions and Intercessions)—and Submission. For this last term some of us feel free at times to substitute the word "Service." One hour of worship may lead up to an act of passive Submission to the will of God. Another time in church may issue in an opportunity to enlist actively for Service. All of this last has to do with the closing prayer.

What a homely device for an educated minister to use in

[1] See Horton Davies, *Christian Worship—Its History and Meaning* (Nashville: Abingdon Press, 1957).

27

preparing for public prayer! Perhaps so! The suggestion comes from the divinity school at Yale, which ought to give the acrostic academic standing. A suggestion of the same kind appeared long ago (1708-10) in Matthew Henry's homiletical commentary, which should commend the idea to other readers. Whatever the source, the term ACTSS shows the basic pattern of public prayers among many Protestants today, as well as in the times of Queen Anne. In any church the use of the acrostic as a check list may raise certain questions. Among the prayers on a given Lord's Day is there serious overlapping? Even more important, is there serious overlooking? In addition to these five elements, is there anything else? If so, that sixth element may deserve no place in Christian prayer.

Why does the acrostic stop with only five aspects of public prayer? The answer comes through a study of church history, starting with Hebrew ways of worship. If any minister wishes to engage in a fascinating pursuit, more and more helpful, let him read with open eyes the prayers reported or recorded in Holy Writ. Let him see if he can find anything other than the five elements that appear in ACTSS. Later, in as far as he has access to the sources, let him do the same with published prayers of churches throughout Christendom, both past and present. He will find that these prayers tend to include only five elements. After such a progressive study of prayers filled with beauty and uplift, he will come away with a new spirit of thankfulness for Christian prayer, and a new feeling of respect for the homely acrostic ACTSS.

Traditions in the Local Church

Conditions in many a local church do not measure up to the ideals of a minister who knows the history of prayer, especially in his own branch of Protestantism. For example, a young man schooled in worthy ways of worship goes from the divinity school to his first charge. There he finds ways of worship different from anything he has learned from books or teachers. "There are more things in heaven and earth, Horatio, than are dreamt of in your philosophy!" In a congregation with a history "ancient and honorable," the incoming pastor may find customs in prayer that seem to him barren and devoid of beauty. Later he may discover that these people really know how to pray in church. Then he begins to thank God.

In a church that has sprung up like a mushroom, another pastor may find something far worse: the lack of traditions and ideals concerning public worship, especially the prayers. In as far as he can judge, many of the people do not take part in the prayers, or seem concerned about wishing to do so. In one congregation, still adolescent, the young minister heard more about the last oyster supper than about the approaching Lord's Supper. In moments of despair he told the Lord that he found as much solemnity and uplift in one occasion as in the other. Gradually he discovered that he could lead the congregation into ways of worship according to the ideals of Holy Scripture.

As a rule, an incoming minister does well to accept what he finds in the way of worship. Whatever the defects in the existing order, or lack of orderly procedure, he can begin at once to make the best of what seems to him a mess. No pattern of worship devised by past individualists or recent experimentalists can prevent a spiritual man from offering public prayers acceptable to God and uplifting to the people. On the other hand, the peace and harmony of the church ought to seem far more important than any improvement in the order of worship or the ways of prayer.

At one church the lay officers in charge of spiritual concerns asked the new minister to guide them into ways of worship consonant with the best ideals of their denomination. He thanked them, but soon he discovered that he did not know the people well enough to proceed with assurance in recommending needed changes. Now that many pastors have begun to think and pray about this portion of their ministry, the new pastor may simply take over what he finds in ways of worship, and thank God for the privilege of following a man who knew how to pray in church.

After a year or so on a new field a minister ought no longer to feel like a stranger, or to seem unaware of changes needed. If loving and patient, kind and tactful, he can take up with the appropriate board of laymen the entire matter of public worship, with special reference to the prayers. Now that he has gained respect and confidence, he ought to seem like a builder, not an iconoclast. Meanwhile he should have studied with care the prevailing customs, so as to retain all that have proved good. As for changes, he may content himself with suggesting only such ways of worship as receive the official endorsement of his denomination. In almost every case, the larger body has approved "for optional use" a "book of public worship," perhaps under a different title.

The changes need include nothing startling, or revolutionary. Often they have to do with such matters as having prayers short rather than long; prayers enough to voice all the vital needs and aspirations of the people; prayers that enable them collectively to take part at intervals not remote from one another; prayers that come at climactic stages, and keep leading the people's hearts upward. All of this, under God, depends

30

far more on the ability and spirituality of the leader than on the sequence of parts in the service. On the other hand, after a minister has tried week after week to lead in an hour of public worship with a hit-and-miss succession of largely unrelated parts, he can testify that the helpfulness of a prayer may depend on what has gone before, and that much of the effectiveness may depend on what comes after.

All these opinions have come out of experience in churches large and small. In a certain congregation more than a hundred years old the incoming pastor had to wait almost a year before he gained the consent of lay officers for the use of the Lord's Prayer in public worship. Later he got permission for women of the church to bring into the House of Prayer each Lord's Day a simple bouquet of home-grown flowers, and for the people to repeat the Apostles' Creed. Fortunately, he had learned from John Henry Jowett's lectures at Yale that a pastor ought never to move on a small majority. "Never take an important step in church life if a large minority is opposed to your proposals." [2]

At present let this mean that a wise pastor waits until he has the hearty approval of the appropriate board. No man in his senses would consult a congregation of any size about their preferences in ways of worship. Alas, there might be "many men of many minds." On the other hand, as a rule, no man ought lightly or unadvisedly to push through any project before the lay officers concerned have come to what Friends term "the sense of the meeting." In the case now before us the young minister learned to value the judgment of those older men, who looked more than once before they took action. Now he thinks of that congregation, under its elderly lay

[2] See *The Preacher: His Life and Work* (New York: Harper & Bros., 1912), pp. 224-27. An inspiring book, full of wisdom. Used by permission.

leadership, as the best church he ever has known, or expects to know on earth.

Those people loved "the holiness of beauty" in public worship. They often praised the prayers of a former minister who saturated his spirit in prayers of the ages, and then echoed their majestic beauty. Neither did anyone object to the new minister's way of following the Christian Year, both in prayers and in preaching. Without using many liturgical terms, in December he could pray and preach about the Incarnation of our Lord; during the period before Easter, Quinquagesima, about the experiences of Christ as He set His face like a flint (Isa. 50:7), going up to Golgotha to die as "the Lamb of God"; and during the period after Easter, about the living Christ, including His Ascension, or else about the Holy Spirit as the power of God in the life of the Church today.

A Guide in Public Worship

Any pastor can secure variety in public prayer by following the general course of the Christian Year. If a layman ever asks why, the minister can refer to the Hebrew Year (Lev. 23), with its variety and climactic progress. Whatever the season, he ought to keep asking: "Am I getting the people to pray, or am I merely saying prayers in their presence?" According to James B. Pratt,[3] the ablest American writer about the psychology of religion, many who attend Protestant services do not pay attention during the prayers, especially the longest one. More of them would give heed if they knew what they were supposed to do at each stage of worship.

Such guidance may come through the weekly bulletin or calendar, whether printed or mimeographed. It may indicate

[3] See The Religious Consciousness (New York: The Macmillan Co., 1921), pp. 303-4.

tersely the aim and character of each successive hymn or prayer. In one bulletin where the order of service did not seem crowded, the names of the prayers appeared as below, each name standing at the center of a line all its own. In the list here, the word "the" has been omitted: Call to United Prayer—Invocation and Confession of Sins—Declaration of Pardon—Prayer of Thanksgiving and Supplication—Lord's Prayer—Consecration of Offerings—Prayer for Illumination —Prayer of Self-Dedication (in another service, Prayer of Enlistment)—and Benediction of Light (or some other phrase to describe a different biblical form of blessing).

Such a statement of purpose and content ought to help every layman and his little ones. Many of them wish to pray with the proper spirit, and with understanding (I Cor. 14: 15a), but they do not know how. Someone may protest that such ideas about public prayer never enter the heads of churchgoers. Alas, this may be a correct version of the facts. If so, why not begin to change their attitude? When they receive the bulletin, why should they not look on it as a guide in the worship of God? If one of them went to a university observatory at night, before he stepped up to the telescope for a view of the rings about Saturn, he would say to the professor in charge: "Tell me, sir, what I am about to see."

This way of giving each hymn or prayer a name ought to have a salutary effect on the leader in worship. In a printed form he obligates himself at each stage to do something specific, something he will not do again in the same hour of worship. A printed order of this kind serves as a promissory note. It calls for prayers almost as pleasing as stars in the Pleiades, where one star differs from all the rest, and each has a beauty all its own. Still they all belong to the same constellation.

The bulletin ought also to indicate the posture expected

during each prayer. Here again, a minister defers to local custom, as interpreted by the appropriate lay officers. Tactfully he can secure their approval of having the people bow down or kneel for every act of prayer. Especially in a congregation with more than a few elderly folk, the hymns and the responsive reading afford sufficient opportunities to stand up and express feeling. As for the prayers, people usually do better to bow down or kneel, with eyes closed. According to Pratt, "The bent knee, the closed eye, and other bodily postures commonly used in worship, have on many a worshiper a decidedly helpful effect in bringing about the religious attitude of mind." [4]

The same writer also insists that we Protestants overemphasize the subjective, or manward, aspects of public worship, most of all in our prayers. "The important thing is not that the worshipers should be able to behold and follow the service or be impressed by it, but that God should be properly and gloriously worshiped." [5] All true! But would it not be more correct, and more Christian, to say that whenever God is "properly and gloriously worshiped," His people are able to follow the service without difficulty, and that by following it they are strongly impressed? In the days of His flesh our Lord spoke of "true worshippers" as those who "worship the Father in spirit and in truth: for the Father seeketh such to worship him" (John 4:23). He still approves the blending of the objective and the subjective, with the objective ever supreme.

Let us agree that public prayers ought to be mainly objective in purpose and largely subjective in effect. As we learn from the Shorter Catechism. "Man's chief end is to glorify God, and to enjoy him forever." To glorify Him in public

[4] Ibid., p. 314.
[5] Ibid., p. 296.

34

worship means in part to make Him better known, and to cause His holy will to be more perfectly done. To enjoy Him in church means to come into His House with gladness, and to worship Him with holy zeal. No congregation ever fails to receive His blessing while worshiping Him aright. Angels of God keep ascending with the praises and prayers of His redeemed children, and descending with blessings from "the Father of all mercies." All of this takes place every Lord's Day in a church where the leader orders his prayers according to a simple pattern, and then forgets about his plans while he leads the people close to the heart of God.

Two Kinds of Public Prayer

Thus far we have been assuming what we ought now to stress. The Lord stands ready to bless two kinds of public prayer. Each has its merits, but the two do not readily mix. One we may call "liturgical," whose excellences are well known. The other we may term "free," which also has much of good, unless liberty descends into license. According to Robert William Dale, John Henry Jowett's scholarly predecessor at Carr's Lane, Birmingham, "It would hardly be possible to inflict a worse injury on the life and work of our Churches than to permit free, extemporaneous prayer to be excluded from our services, or even relegated to an inferior position. We too have received the Holy Ghost."

In his noteworthy series of Yale Lectures, Dale opens up his heart by telling about his early experience in learning to lead in public prayer.

The root of my difficulties . . . was a mistaken impression that extemporaneous prayer might include—in addition to its own excellences—the characteristic excellences of a liturgy. But we must make our choice. In extemporaneous prayer the stateliness, the majesty, the aesthetic beauty of such a service as that of the Anglican Episcopal Church, and the power which it derives from venerable associations, are impossible. We must be content with simplicity, directness, pathos, reverence, fervor. If we are less vividly conscious than those who use a liturgy that we are walking in the footsteps of the saints of other centuries, we may find compensation in a closer and more direct relation to the actual life of the men, women, and children who are waiting with ourselves for the mercy and help and pity of God.[6]

By "extemporaneous prayer" Dale means what is carefully prepared in substance, but not in form. He would agree that our mistakes often come from trying in a single prayer to combine the two sorts of excellence. No man, however gifted, can pray well in two different ways at the same time. So why do we ever make a hodgepodge and call it a prayer? On the contrary, we should feel free to use at will any form of sound words taken over from the past. If we are wise, we shall let any such thing of beauty stand by itself. At other times in public worship we should give a worthy place to free prayer. As for the proportion between the two elements in any service, the Holy Spirit stands ready to guide the minister who sets himself to do what will bring glory to God and blessing to those who worship Him.

The majority of recent books on public worship plead for a larger use of liturgical prayers. On the contrary, a discerning word has come from an Anglican scholar, B. H. Streeter, of Oxford. He made a long and careful study of public prayers, both ancient and modern. After an able statement of many excellences and some possible weaknesses in liturgical prayer,

[6] *Nine Lectures on Preaching* (New York: George H. Doran Co., 1878), pp. 264-65.

he wrote appreciatively about our way of drawing near to God in "free prayer":

> Its outstanding merit is of course its complete freedom and adaptability. Given a minister of real spirituality and a gift of devotional expression (two things that do not necessarily always go together), the congregation is little likely to be listless and inattentive. . . . The whole service takes on an individual cast, in strong contrast to the stereotyped and, to the young and uneducated, seemingly artificial character of a liturgical service.

Then Streeter points out the main weakness of "free prayer":

> Its great defect is the demand it makes on the personality and powers of the minister. Where the minister is a man of very exceptional gifts, I believe this type of service elicits far more real response in the way of active participation in worship than the Anglican Offices. Where he is an average man, I doubt whether there is in practice much to choose between the two types. But where he is even a little below the average, either of spirituality, culture, or gift of expression, I believe it is distinctly less satisfactory than a fixed Liturgy.[7]

So it seems that a man of ability, properly educated for his lifework, should have no insuperable difficulty in the use of free prayer. Also, he should feel at home among prayers handed down from other days. If so, he can bring forth from his treasure stores of devotion things both new and old. In all such holy concerns, rules can have little place. Even so, two suggestions will appear later in this book. First, on a momentous occasion, such as the dedication of a new church edifice,

[7] *Concerning Prayer* (London: Macmillan & Co. Ltd., 1916), pp. 285-86. Used by permission.

the order of worship may call for more of the liturgical element than in a regular service. Second, from week to week the liturgical element is more likely to appear early in worship, which is largely objective, than in the latter part, which is more subjective. In all these matters a wise man follows the guidance of the Holy Spirit in response to specific prayer.

CHAPTER III

Beginning a
Morning Service

AN HOUR OF MORNING WORSHIP NORMALLY BEGINS WITH MUSIC from the organ. As an act of worship, in the spirit of prayer, and not merely as a preliminary to something more important, the Organ Prelude ought to commence before the people assemble, perhaps fifteen minutes before any worship with words. If soft and meditative, because prayerful, the Prelude helps to "condition the desired response." From the moment of entrance into the House of Prayer every worshiper ought to feel that God is present, and that He desires the undivided attention of everyone in church. If the organist attempted to show artistic mastery of a complicated musical instrument, or tried to imitate a thunderstorm, many people might start to talk, perhaps about the instrument and the organist. But if the sacred music seems to come down softly from above, everyone ought to sense the need of silence. "Be still, and know that I am God." (Ps. 46:10.)

A Call for United Prayer

After the Organ Prelude may come the Call to Worship. Since the people have already been engaged in silent worship, it would be more fitting to have a Call to Praise God. This

Call may be sung by the choir, or spoken by the minister. Then may follow a hymn by the congregation, or some other choral ascription of praise. Whatever the plan, these first moments of vocal worship ought to be corporate. "All one body we!" Later in the hour, especially toward the end, the stress may fall on each person and his relation to God. At the beginning the minister wishes to merge all the people into one worshiping family of God. These opening words ought to set the "tone color" for the entire service.

Instead of a Call to Praise God, some of us prefer a Call to United Prayer. The vocal worship may begin with holy song, either by the congregation or from the choir. Then the minister utters his Call to United Prayer. The Call usually consists of a verse or two from a single portion of the Bible. These words the leader commits to memory, and speaks from heart to heart, and eye to eye, without looking down to refresh his recollection. In Holy Scripture such passages abound. Even if one omits passages that call for praise, and those that concern a single person, one can make a large enough collection of calls to united prayer.

The list that follows will show some of the possibilities, but not all. In any one case the selection of a passage ought to depend on the season of the year, and the nature of the occasion. After six months or so a pastor can repeat the same Call. As with first-class hymns, the proper use of beautiful words from Holy Writ never suffers from occasional repetition, if intelligent. Some of us do not let six months go by without having the people sing "Now thank we all our God," and "When I survey the wondrous cross." In like manner we often use our favorite biblical calls to united prayer. But it would be a pity if anyone in church got the idea that there was only one such call, or if he thought there was only one first-class hymn of a certain kind. Both with hymns and calls to prayer, the leader in worship ought to have a treasure house, filled with words of beauty and uplifting power. Any such list of calls to united prayer should include the following:

Ps. 24:3-5	Isa. 1:18	Matt. 11:28-30
Ps. 27:14	Isa. 55:6-7	Matt. 18:19
Ps. 34:15	Jer. 29:11-13	Luke 1:78b-79
Ps. 37:5-6	Lam. 3:22-23	Luke 11:13
Ps. 46:10	Hos. 6:1-3	Phil. 4:6-7
Ps. 55:22	Hos. 14:1-2	Heb. 4:14-16
Ps. 95:6-7a	Joel 2:12-13	Jas. 4:8
Ps. 124:8	Hab. 2:20	I Pet. 5:6-7
Ps. 145:18-19	Matt. 7:7-8	I John 5:14-15

In the Call to United Prayer the minister addresses the people. At other times during the hour he should feel free to employ the first person, either plural or singular. Here, in the name of the Lord, he voices a kind of imperative, not as a stern command, but as a joyous appeal. He does not say: "I will lift up mine eyes unto the hills" (Ps. 121:1), or, "I was glad when they said unto me, Let us go into the house of the Lord" (122:1). Neither does he try to teach or exhort: "They that wait upon the Lord shall renew their strength" (Isa. 40: 31). If the order of service does not bid the people bow down or kneel, he ought not to say: "O come, let us worship and bow down; let us kneel before the Lord our Maker" (Ps. 95: 6). Whatever the choice of beautiful words, the pastor uses them in calling the people to pray together as a family of God's redeemed children.

The Prayer of Adoration

After the Call the minister leads in an Adoring Invocation. Before the Invocation, if the people have been standing to sing, they kneel or bow down. The spirit of the brief Invocation may be that of Isaiah's vision: "Holy, holy, holy, is the Lord of hosts; the whole earth is full of his glory" (Isa. 6:3b). This opening prayer the minister often finds hard to voice in church. At this stage of worship, being human, he may not feel ready to express adoration. He may know that many of the people are thinking more about themselves and their moods than about God and His glory.

Fortunately, this act of adoration need not continue long. In the Alps when a traveler first looks up from afar and beholds the Matterhorn resting in splendor beneath sunlit snow, he may utter only a few words from a heart full of awe and wonder. In the House of Prayer the worshipers rightly expect the minister to voice their feelings in the presence of the One who created the Alps, and the sun that shines on the snow. At best the Adoring Invocation leads worshipers to feel "lost in wonder, love, and praise."

In other days a lover of beauty returned from a tour of the Continent and Britain. In reply to an inquiry about his most memorable experience, he told about the prayer with which Spurgeon began his part of worship in the London Tabernacle. Not every minister has such a gift for expression of exalted feelings Godward. Even a man with a poetic soul may find that his spirits flag. If so, he may turn to his treasury of prayers from other days. There he should find what he desires in the way of holy aspiration. For example, take this familiar collect from the third century:

Almighty God, unto whom all hearts are open, all desires known, and from whom no secrets are hid; Cleanse the thoughts of our hearts by the inspiration of Thy Holy Spirit, that we may perfectly love Thee, and worthily magnify Thy holy name; through Jesus Christ our Lord. Amen.

The Confession of Sins

In an ideal order of worship the Invocation, however brief, would stand alone. In many churches there seems to be early in the hour no other place for the Confession of Sins. So this may come after the Invocation, with only a slight pause between, and with a change of tone, which becomes more somber. As in the experience of young Isaiah at worship, a sense of God's holiness ought to produce a feeling of unworthiness: "Woe is me! for I am undone, because I am a man of unclean lips, and I dwell in the midst of a people of unclean lips: for mine eyes have seen the King, the Lord of hosts" (Isa. 6:5).

What Isaiah felt in the way of contrition and shame, the people in church ought to feel when they behold the goodness of God. These feelings the pastor may voice in words of his own, words few in number and memorable in form. Or he may turn, once again, to his storehouse of prayers. There he should find more than one suitable form of confession, which shows the meaning of an old phrase, *multum in parvo*. As with the brief Adoration, the Prayer of Confession need include nothing local and temporary. Hence the leader may at times resort to the use of borrowed forms. Fortunately, the laws of copyright do not apply to such use of prayers from other men and churches.

In more than one congregation without prescribed forms of prayer the appropriate lay officers permit the corporate use of a few confessions, frankly borrowed. For such use three or four forms of confession may be printed or mimeographed and pasted on blank spaces in the back of the hymnal. If so, each form may have a number. Then the bulletin may call for Confession of Sins (I), (II), or (III). The idea is that with no announcement the people can unite in humble prayer of contrition, with a fervent plea for pardon, cleansing, and peace.

The first form of Confession may be that in the Anglican and the Methodist way of worship, beginning: "Almighty and most merciful Father, we have erred and strayed from thy ways like lost sheep." The second, from the Presbyterian *Book of Common Worship*, commencing: "Most holy and merciful Father; We acknowledge and confess before Thee; Our sinful nature prone to evil and slothful in good." The third, from the Scottish *Book of Common Order*, shows how to combine a brief prayer of Adoration with a form of Confession. Here follow the first two paragraphs, which would be long enough for the purpose in view:

O eternal God, mighty in power and of majesty ineffable, whose Name is great, and whose goodness passeth knowledge, to Thee alone be praise and adoration from the hosts of heaven and all who dwell upon the earth.

We humble ourselves in Thy presence, confessing our unworthiness and sin. We have not sought first Thy Kingdom and righteousness; we have been fretful and troubled about many things, and have neglected those that are needful to our peace. We have not loved our neighbor as ourselves, nor always done to others as we would that they should do to us. We have yielded to temptation; the sin we should have hated we have committed in Thy sight. Most gracious God, our heavenly Father, forgive us, we entreat Thee. Cleanse us from all unrighteousness, and renew a right spirit within us, through the grace of our Redeemer, Jesus Christ. Amen.[1]

[1] (London: Oxford University Press, 1928), p. 12. From *The Book of Common Order* by permission of the Church of Scotland Committee on Public Worship and Aids to Devotion.

The first part is spoken by the minister, and need not appear in the printed or mimeographed form. The second part is said by the people in unison with the leader. The paragraph shows the form that such a prayer may well assume. This one keeps close to reality, as it appears in Holy Writ, and still reflects the experiences of countless folk. Something of the sort people ought to confess every Lord's Day. By using at times a few such borrowed forms, and at other times similar words of his own, a pastor can secure the sort of variety and uplift that often seems wanting in this part of worship from week to week, and from year to year.

The Declaration of Pardon

Such a Confession would seem incomplete if it did not lead up to a Declaration of Pardon. After the people have voiced their sorrow for sin, the minister pauses for a moment, and then assures them that the Lord has forgiven all the sins they have rightly confessed. In this Declaration the pastor may use words of his own. If so, they may center round a well-known verse from the Bible, such as: "If we confess our sins, he is faithful and just to forgive us our sins, and to cleanse us from all unrighteousness" (I John 1:9). Then he may point to the basis for such assurance: "The blood of Jesus Christ his Son cleanseth us from all sin" (1:7).

At another hour of worship the leader may use a form of assurance taken from his denominational guidebook, or from some other. The one that follows comes from the Presbyterian *Book of Common Worship.* This form avoids the use of any word suggesting "absolution." We who follow Luther and Calvin back to the Scriptures for ideals of public prayer cannot sanction absolution of sins by anyone but God. On the other hand, we ought to show His readiness to do away with

45

all the transgressions that His people sincerely confess, and
for which they humbly ask His pardon.

This Bible point of view appears in an "Order of Worship"
adapted from "The Sunday Service of John Wesley," and
"suggested for occasional use" in the Methodist Church. All
of this appears in their official hymnal. After a Call to Confession, by the minister, with the people standing, they all
bow down or kneel to join with him in the printed General
Confession, which has come from the Anglican Church. Then
the pastor voices a Prayer for Pardon:

O Lord, we beseech Thee, absolve Thy people from their
offenses; that, through Thy bountiful goodness, we may be delivered from the bonds of those sins which by our frailty we have
committed. Grant this, O Heavenly Father, for Jesus Christ's
sake, our blessed Lord and Saviour. Amen.[2]

Whatever the form, the public Confession of Sins ought to
issue in the sort of assurance that will dominate the rest of
the morning service. When once the local representative of
God has voiced a Declaration of Pardon for all who here do
truly repent and confess, he should not in the same hour of
worship ask for the pardon of the very same sins. On a level
purely human, how would a Godly mother feel if her little son
asked and secured pardon for an offense, and then kept coming back pleading for pardon because of the same offense?
And yet, if unprepared, a leader in worship may in a single
service confess the same sins five or six times, with never a
suggestion that the Lord delights to forgive. What a way to
misrepresent the "God of all mercy"!

These acts of prayer at the beginning of morning worship

[2] See *The Methodist Hymnal* (Nashville: The Methodist Publishing
House, 1939), pp. 506-7.

may seem to consume precious minutes. If so, the fault lies with the description. In practice, a minister can carry out any one of these suggestions in ninety seconds. Speaking deliberately, at about 130 words a minute, he can have a Call to United Prayer (a brief pause), a short Invocation (pause), a Confession of Sins (pause), and a Declaration of Pardon—all in less than two minutes. How could pastor and people spend this much of God's time more profitably? Have we Americans come to a stage in church history when the chief purpose of public worship is to get through and go home?

On the other hand, the spiritual value of these opening prayers depends on their prominence, not on their length. If fairly deliberate, and not long, each part is likely to enlist the active participation of every worshiper. Week after week, if people receive the glad assurance that the Lord has forgiven all their sins, they will not deliberately come to church ten or fifteen minutes late.

The discussion so far seems to have bypassed two important parts of morning worship. In many churches the vocal service begins with the Doxology, followed by the Invocation and the Lord's Prayer. Surely no one would discount the value of the Doxology and the Lord's Prayer, in both of which the congregation as a whole takes part, and that with vigor. The present suggestion calls for the Doxology at a climactic stage, when lay officers bring forward the gifts of the waiting throng, and for the Lord's Prayer at the end of the Pastoral Prayer. At each of these climactic stages the people might otherwise keep silent, when they ought to speak forth words of praise.

According to our acrostic, ACTSS, the corporate Confession of Sins ought to precede the thanksgiving that rings out in the Doxology. After the Pastoral Prayer, in which they do not as a rule take any audible part, the people should be ready to join heartily in the Lord's Prayer. In sixty-seven words, notable for simplicity and strength, the Lord's Prayer gathers up and presents before God the substance of all that pastor and people together have said to Him so far in their morning sacrifices of praise and prayer. So it seems that the opening parts of morning worship need the careful attention of the leader, always in the spirit of prayer.

CHAPTER IV

Offering a
General Prayer

Now we come to the most important regular public prayer. By common consent it has become known as the Pastoral Prayer. In a high sense all the prayers by a minister in church ought to be pastoral. So let us think of this longest one as the "General Prayer," a term suggested by the present-day emphasis on General Education. In many a congregation the heart of the Lord's undershepherd finds its fullest expression in this act of oblation. In as far as the people later recall the prayers of God's House, they think of this one more than all the others.

In recent days the General Prayer is sometimes missing, or else it lacks essential elements. With the zeal to get through on time, and to "enrich the service" with many other things, there seems to be little time left for Thanksgivings, Petitions, and Intercessions. In such a church the laymen may sense the lack of something, they scarcely know what. Surely no one wishes to have long prayers, or long services, but no less surely the prayers in church ought to express the vital needs and the aspirations of the persons present.

A worthy pastor senses the importance of the General Prayer. At the close of a long and fruitful ministry, much of it in the pastorate, the president of a theological seminary declares that he thinks he has accomplished almost as much for God through pastoral prayers as through sermons. He feels that the two belong together in spirit, as inseparably as warmth and heat that proceed from the same sun in December. He feels, too, that a young pastor makes a grievous mistake when he prepares for pulpit announcements more carefully than for prayers, and in church devotes more time to announcements than to oblations. Where has God promised to bless the ordinary run of announcements in church? Why not save time here?

While not so brief, the General Prayer may present fewer difficulties than the Invocation. After fifteen minutes or so of public worship, both minister and people may feel more in the spirit of prayer. The pastor, if faithful to his work, knows the heart needs and longings of the people. They have found that he can voice aspirations they never have felt able to express. In fact, this part of a minister's privileges may in time seem to him unduly easy. Knowing that the spiritual needs of worshipers continue to be much the same from week to week, he may fall into a self-made routine that deepens into a rut. With much the same elements, in the same order, and with the same words, his "long prayer" may become so stereotyped that any intelligent layman could repeat it from memory, word for word, if he thought it worth remembering and repeating.

Such a "long prayer" tends to grow by accretion. Only a man of genius can pray long and profitably in church week after week. Even if he could, a man of wisdom would not do so today. Spurgeon often prayed fifteen minutes, but he had no choir to sing anthems, and no organ for other sacred music. Cotton Mather once held forth for seventy-five minutes. Samuel Terrey continued in a single prayer for 120, which must have seemed many more. Today a wise man of God never thinks of a "long" prayer, or refers to it in public. For the longest one in church he may look on three minutes as normal, with five as the upper limit.

An occasional young minister, straight from the seminary, may wonder how he can keep going, week after week, for three whole minutes. A few years later, people may wonder why he speeds past convenient stopping places where they could find refreshment for weary souls. Meanwhile some of them do not try to pray. They may have begun to find fault with the pastor for lack of terminal facilities. They could follow him more easily if he made clear the successive stages in the General Prayer. At the beginning, something like this: "Let us give thanks to God." Later, "Let us pray for those here present." Toward the end, "Let us intercede for others elsewhere." During each part the leader need address the Deity only once, each time with a different name.

A Time for Thanksgiving

The content of the thanksgivings usually depends in part on what has gone before. If this prayer follows immediately after the Scripture Lesson, the pastor may unintentionally interpret and enforce what he has read. If so, he is trying to teach. Even if he prays only to God, this conventional order of service calls for the same leading voice in two successive acts most important in worship. Wisdom seems to suggest more of an alternating order, in which the Lord speaks through His written Word, and the people respond in holy song.

Many of us prefer to have a hymn after the Scripture Lesson. If local custom does not permit this, the lay officers will sanction some other kind of choral response, either by the choir or by the people, preferably the latter. In some churches they rise to sing the Gloria in Excelsis Deo. Elsewhere a congregation stands to join in the Apostles' Creed. At some places they do both, in the order above. Whatever the form of the response, the people ought to express their feelings, heartily, before they bow down or kneel for prayers of thanksgiving.

The order of the thanksgivings may resemble that of Psalm 103, though it is not a prayer. The sacred poet begins with blessings that concern one person. Then the words of gratitude reach out to include other circles, each wider than the one before, until at last praises sound forth from angelic hosts. In an occasional prayer today, the leader may begin with blessings on the nation. In celebrating some notable anniversary, such as the birth of our country, or the founding of a venerable church, that event would come first in the thanksgivings. As a rule in prayer, as in preaching, a man does well to begin with the people where they are. Rightly or wrongly, at this stage in public worship, nine times out of ten every man present thinks first and most about himself. If so, why not start there?

Let us give thanks to God: for life, for health, for strength; for the use of reason and senses; for home, for church, for native land; for answered prayers, for recovered health, and for peace of heart.

So the prayer of thanksgiving may proceed for about sixty seconds. In that time, speaking deliberately, a minister can include many personal reasons for gratitude to God. He has not time to start sentence after sentence with any self-made formula, such as: "We thank Thee, O Lord, for this beautiful morning." Instead of indulging in "meaningless repetitions" of things already obvious, he does well to pray directly about persons. Either in the thanksgivings, or else in the petitions that follow, the man with a shepherd heart speaks on behalf of every person, or group of persons, here waiting before God.

Without any mention of names, one can utter thanksgivings that are personal. Instead of thanking the Lord for a hypothetical home, one can voice gratitude for the little boy or girl, and the newborn baby like the Holy Child Jesus; for the growing lad or lass, coming to know the Lord in the beauty of life's morning; for the youth or maiden, standing on the threshold of life, and striving to become like the young Man of Galilee; for the man or woman in the "middle passage of the years"; for the aged saint, sitting by the western window, waiting for the end of life's little day on earth; and for the memory of a beloved grandfather who has heard the sound of the trumpet, and has passed beyond the river that men call death.

Thanksgivings ought to vary from week to week. The basic order may continue much the same, with ever-widening circles, but the content ought to vary according to the season of the year, and the local condition of the times. Negatively, there is one proviso: the leader ought to leave out any item that should not concern the entire congregation, and that should not call for public thanksgiving to God. In short, thanksgivings ought to be personal, rather than abstract; and about persons with flesh and blood, not about such present-day impersonalities as "man," "mankind," and "humanity."

Occasionally, for variety, a minister can have a prayer of thanksgiving by the congregation in unison. If the bulletin permits enough space, he can have printed the "General

Thanksgiving" from the Book of Common Prayer. This prayer begins: "Almighty God, Father of all mercies; we Thine unworthy servants; Do give Thee most humble and hearty thanks; For all Thy goodness and loving-kindness to us and to all men." The following prayer of thanksgiving comes from John Watson, "Ian Maclaren," who was reputed to be the most beloved pastor of his day in Liverpool, if not in Britain:

Heavenly Father, who art the Giver of every good and perfect gift, we thank Thee for our creation in Thine image, for Thy preserving mercy through all the days of our [lives], for the comfort and protection of our homes, for all who love us and whom we love, for healing in sickness, for deliverance in danger and comfort in sorrow, for the work given us to do and the strength wherewith to do it, and for the innumerable mercies of Thy mindful providence; and above all, for the coming of Thy beloved Son into the world, for the gracious words He spoke, for the merciful work He did, for His bitter passion and atoning sacrifice on the Cross, and for His mighty Resurrection from the dead; for the pardon of sins, the means of grace, the indwelling of Thy Spirit, and the life everlasting. Amen.

A Place for Petitions

After a brief pause, the minister voices the needs and desires of those present in church. Here he may feel sure of a still more immediate concern than in the thanksgivings. As a Christian optimist he has expressed such feelings of gratitude as ought to well up in the hearts of God's redeemed children. As a Christian realist he knows that many of them have not yet attained perfection, and that they think less about the goodness of God than about what seems to be lacking in their own hearts and homes. Even the least selfish layman in church has personal needs and desires about which the minister ought to feel concern.

On Saturday morning the leader makes ready for the General Prayer. He may recall a friend who feels unduly concerned about an operation soon to come; another whose daughter has gone to the state hospital, with little prospect of ever returning home; a third whose life has been shadowed by a new and sudden sorrow; a fourth whose sadness has stretched out over twenty years, and seems to be growing worse. So the list may keep mounting up, to include the unwilling victim of fear, anxiety, or loneliness; of discouragement, disillusionment, or despair; of an inferiority complex, or a tendency to doubt. Last of all, and far from least, the one who exists beneath the shadow of unforgiven sins, and has not yet found peace through acceptance of Christ and His redeeming grace.

All these needs, and others like them, prevail among mortals who come to church. Still other occasions for petition vary according to the season, and the state of the times, here at home. Hence the leader ought to single out specific needs that he will present before God on the morrow, and decide which ones he will tomorrow leave unspoken. One need he ought never to ignore or pass over lightly: that of a person who lacks calm and radiant assurance about the reality of life beyond. A painting of the Madonna and Child by Raphael always shows a glimpse of the sky. So these petitions on the Lord's Day should lead to at least a glimpse of light from the unseen City of God.

A Christlike pastor knows how to pray in terms of one person; it may be one of many. Because of their corporate character and purpose, prayers early in the service keep away from reference to any one person. But when he makes ready

for the General Prayer, the minister ought to remember that
loneliness, as a rule, does not concern people in the plural.
According to the Gospels, our Lord usually dealt with such
matters as they related to one person at a time. So did the
psalmist: "Why art thou cast down, O my soul?" (42:5a).
In a downtown church of Los Angeles one night a minister
prayed for "the girl who buried her mother last week." After
the service three young women tarried to thank him, and to
ask how he knew about their sorrow. Such a petition might
seem out of place elsewhere, but it shows how a discerning
minister adapts his prayers to the needs of the hour. This
pastor, Roy L. Smith, looks on the General Prayer as perhaps
the most important part of worship in a downtown church
at night.

In a minute or so of petitions no leader can voice all the
heart needs and desires of any congregation. Every week he
has to select certain items and pass by others. Even at best
he feels a sense of incompleteness, and so do some of the
people. Hence the time for petitions may lead up to a brief
period of silence. The organist ought to know in advance, so
that she will not improvise something musical to make up
for the leader's "loss of memory." In the midst of a prayer,
silence ought to mean absence of sound, except the beating
of a heart that seems ready to burst. "Be still, and know that
I am God." (Ps. 46:10.)

Before he asks for such a period of silence in church, the
minister ought to feel sure of the right response. In more than
one congregation such an "innovation" might cause a temporary tempest. Some of the "saints" feel strongly that they
"pay the parson to do their praying in public." In time, for
the sake of young people, older folk should learn to endure,
if not to enjoy, periods of silence. They will accept the change

more complacently if they know about it in advance than if they enter into the experience without tactful preparation.

All of us wish to enlist young folk for regular attendance at church and for hearty participation in worship. The "problem" does not permit any cheap and easy solution. One thing we ought to know: many young people do not enjoy our traditional ways of prayer, especially what they term the "long one." To them it seems like a ministerial monologue. At college or at a summer conference some of them have learned to think of prayer, and of preaching, as "co-operative." The most mature may look on public prayer as "existential," which refers to a soul in a crisis, groping out after the God who seems to hide Himself. For example, think of young Isaiah in the House of Prayer. Would he have come out on the Lord's side if some older person had kept talking to God all the time? As for possible alternatives to long pastoral soliloquies, we shall return to the subject later.

The Call for Intercessions

The General Prayer leads up climactically to intercessions for persons and causes beyond the congregation and its members. The glory of Christianity consists largely in its world view. If one were asked to sum up the Christian philosophy of life on the human level, he could do no better than echo the answer of General William Booth: "Others!" In public prayers for others the home pastor shows the breadth or the narrowness of his human interests. Does he care about the hungry waifs of India as much as he cares about underprivileged children here at home? In brief, does he care about others, or only about himself and the home church?

Usually the intercessions begin with the local community. These need not be many, or long. Week after week a minister can single out some different person or group for whom the home church ought to pray. Here follow certain examples.

Under God, the welfare of many little boys and girls depends on His blessing the mayor, the policeman on his beat, the fireman at his post, the physician on his rounds, or the teacher at her desk. As for special causes, occasionally a minister can pray briefly about the Community Chest or the Red Cross, the need for rain, or relief after a flood. In a wider circle he can intercede much more often for the Chief Magistrate. If the people think he belongs to "the wrong political party," they feel that he needs prayers all the more! Without serving as a partisan propagandist, the minister can remember before God the victims of race prejudice, or any others whose welfare has to do with the advancement of the Kingdom in our land today.

The climactic stage ought to come in prayers for World Missions and World Peace. Here, too, the pastor needs to be adequately informed. If he merely says, "God bless India," or "Remember Japan," he may as well save that much time. Like the Lord his God, the minister ought to love the world, but not always wholesale. If the denomination supports workers in thirteen countries overseas, he may on each Sunday intercede for the workers in one of those lands. The purpose is not to educate the people about denominational missions, or to increase their giving for benevolences, but to voice the desires of local believers for the coming of the Kingdom in every land for which the Redeemer died, and over which He longs to rule.

The Need for Two Prayers

A glance back over this chapter will make clear that the General Prayer includes too many elements, each of them important. Consequently, as a rule, it seems too "general." If a wise minister has his way, he arranges for two prayers instead of one. First, "A Prayer of Thanksgiving," all by itself, about a minute long. A little later, "A Prayer of Supplication," perhaps two minutes. This includes petitions for those present, and intercessions for others elsewhere. Both prayers ought to be terse and selective. In Holy Scripture, with all its wealth and variety of public prayers, it would be hard to find one that "covers everything and touches nothing." With the exception of Solomon's words at the dedication of the Temple (I Kings 8:23-51), the prayers in the Bible tend to be short. Once in a lifetime, on a momentous occasion, a pastor may feel moved to pray more at length, but as a rule he accomplishes most for God when he stops within three minutes.

Perhaps unfortunately, many churchgoers today have motion-picture minds, and television tendencies. Outside church they do not learn to concentrate. Partly for this reason, other things being equal, a short prayer makes more of an appeal, and more of a permanent impression, than a long one. In Chicago a well-known pastor of a large church reports that when past fifty years of age, he began to prepare carefully for his public prayers. As a consequence he worked on the General Prayer four times as long as in earlier years, and then the prayer itself lasted only half as long as previously. "Use not vain repetitions, as the heathen do: for they think that they shall be heard for their much speaking." (Matt 6:7.)

CHAPTER V

Blessing the
People's Gifts

THE PRAYER AT THE TIME OF THE OFFERING DESERVES MORE
attention than many of us give. Somehow we should lead the
people to look on the offering as an important act of public
worship. Undergirding it lies the biblical teaching about
stewardship. This term may originally have served a holy
purpose, but of late it has lost its luster. People today associate
the term "steward" with a more or less efficient underling
who deals with food and drink on a Pullman dining car, and
has little power. Even on an airplane, where a charming
stewardess pleases everyone, she has authority only in minor
matters. And yet in church we keep asking strong men and
women of affairs to look on themselves as God's subordi-
nate servants, who have no minds of their own, and make no
important decisions about the support of the most important work in the world!

The word "trusteeship" would convey the Bible meaning
about the use of money, and would lead to no unpleasant con-
notations. Churchgoers think of a trustee as a person of consequence, in charge of important business for the local congregation, or of some important concerns for others. The
trustees of a church, of a bank, or of an estate must make

vital decisions. So must every Christian who looks on himself as God's trustee, appointed to supervise the money that passes through his hands in business or at home. All of this has to do with the teaching ministry of the local church. At present we can think only about the way the pastor and others should receive the gifts that God's other trustees bring to Him for His blessing.

How can a minister help make the presentation of the offering a memorable act of worship, and not merely a way of securing money enough to pay the bills for heat and light? Privately he may encourage the lay officers to entrust the public receiving of God's money to responsible men, not to beardless youths. He may suggest that the men in charge move with dignity, and not make haste as though they were marching out to war. He can also arrange with the leader of the choir to help make this act of oblation memorable. "Let all things be done decorously and in order." (I Cor. 14:40 Moffatt.)

A Climactic Part of Worship

By tactful leadership the minister can make the presentation of "tithes and offerings" a church event, not a passing incident. Instead of letting people think of public giving as a duty to be done grudgingly, he can lead them to regard it as a joyous morning sacrifice to God. People with a Hebrew background refer to such giving as a "peace offering," which corresponds to what we call a "thank offering." How different from the present-day stress on self-denial, as though that were the pinnacle of Christian virtue! Sometimes we even urge God's redeemed children to "give until it hurts." We might as well adopt the slogan of the streets: "The life you save may be your own." How pagan!

The picture may seem to be overdrawn. If so, read the bulletins of many a church for a month or two. Also listen to the announcements just before the morning offering, and notice how some of them interrupt the public worship of God. Like the poor, such announcements seem to be ever with us. Through the lay officers the pastor can secure the adoption of a plan that operates where God's people worship Him continuously from the beginning of the Prelude to the end of the Postlude. This plan makes no provision for announcements, other than those that appear in the bulletin. In case of an emergency, the pastor may disregard the rule. Even then he announces only such times of worship as concern the entire congregation, and such as warrant the blessing of God.

These ideals would also rule out much so-called humor. A few minutes before a certain pastor led the people in celebrating the Lord's Supper, he broke into the service to say: "I forgot to announce a special collection today for the Old People's Home at Middletown. You fellows had better dig down into your jeans and bring out a lot of dough, because you may be there yourselves one of these days." Then some of the people laughed, and others wanted to weep, because their minister had shown a dislocated sense of humor. Even on the high day of the quarterly Communion he had tried to serve the Lord with the jawbone of an ass. Ministerial humor has its place, but not in the Holy of Holies.

Whatever the arrangements concerning announcements, there should be a Call to Worship by Giving. The leader may employ such words as these: "Let us worship God with our tithes and offerings." Thus he assumes that present-day Christians ought to give as largely as old-time Hebrews. At least ideally, they looked on the tithe as a minimum, to which they added freewill offerings. After the Call to Give there may be a verse of Scripture. If so, the passage ought to vary from week to week. These few words from the Bible resemble the earlier Call to United Prayer. In each case the minister addresses the people. He plans to speak kindly and expectantly, never apologetically or mandatorily. He appeals, but he does not demand.

In calling for gifts, the minister acts as the personal representative of God. Not as a beggar pleading for a dole, but as a spokesman for the most important enterprise in the world, he speaks with authority from God. Not reading from a book, but speaking from the heart, he summons the people to their high privilege of helping support the work of the Kingdom. In selecting a verse for the day, he gives the preference to words of beauty that sing their way into men's souls, and then keep echoing there. Here follows a list that shows a variety of scriptural appeals for giving as an act of corporate worship:

Ps. 24:1	Prov. 3:9	Acts 20:35b
Ps. 50:14	Mal. 3:10	II Cor. 8:7
Ps. 76:11	Matt. 6:19-21	II Cor. 8:9
Ps. 96:8	Luke 6:38	II Cor. 9:8

After the Call for United Giving the minister conforms with local custom. If it leads him to handle the plates, he moves deliberately, with both hands grasping each plate, or tier of plates. In conference with the Music Committee he arranges for worshipful organ music during the reception of the people's gifts. If the organist later asks what he means by worshipful music, he may refer to Bach's "Jesus, Thou Joy of Man's Desiring." As for an anthem by the choir he prefers

63

that the choral music come at another time, but he welcomes the right sort of choral response by the people or the choir after the prayer that attends the offering. The regulating idea is that during any important act of worship the people should be doing only one thing. If they attempted to do two things at once, they would feel that neither was vital.

A Prayer Before the Offering

In more than a few churches the order of service calls for a brief prayer before the offering. After the minister asks for this act of worship, the organist plays inconspicuous music and the appointed receivers come forward to stand facing the pastor. While they hold the plates soon to be filled with gifts of love, he utters a sentence or two of prayer for the people who are waiting to give. He may prefer that the prayer come after the reception of the gifts, so as to call for the consecration of substance, but in all such matters of detail, involving no principle of right or wrong, he conforms with local custom.

The spirit of this prayer before the offering may resemble that of a little boy at the dinner table. Before the members of the household break bread together, he may utter an old-time prayer: "Lord, make us grateful for what we are about to receive." Like that blessing in a home, this prayer in church may mean much or little, according to the wisdom and the care of the one who speaks to God. Instead of letting his prayer seem like a conventional gesture, to which no one gives more than a passing thought, the pastor can make this part of worship seem memorable.

The dominant note should be that of self-dedication. The spirit of the pastor ought to be that of the apostle Paul. When writing to friends in a distant city church, he said: "I

64

seek not yours, but you" (II Cor. 12:14b). Of course he wished them to contribute bountifully, as the Lord had prospered them. But he felt more concern about the dedication of the givers than about the amount of their offerings. As a wise leader of men and churches he knew that if the people first gave themselves to God, they would respond generously to every opportunity for contributing to His work. "The gift without the giver is bare." The Apostle also knew that the best way to bring about self-dedication to God was to stress His goodness in sending His Son to die for our sins. Surely our self-giving ought to be like that of God.

Often the minister's prayer simply echoes the biblical Call for Giving. He does not attempt to explain and enforce the verse. He thanks God for what it promises, and then pleads for its fulfillment in the lives of this people. For instance, he may have quoted from memory the prophet's words about God's opening the windows of heaven to bless those who give willingly (Mal. 3:10). Then the prayer voices thanks for the outpouring of His mercies on those present, and invokes His blessing on them as generous givers. At another time he quotes the verse that many of us employ too exclusively at such a time: "Remember the words of the Lord Jesus, how he said, It is more blessed to give than to receive" (Acts 20:35b). Then the brief prayer has to do with God's gifts and our response:

Heavenly Father, in mercy Thou hast given us countless tokens of Thy favor. Thou hast even sent Thy Son as the unspeakable Gift of Thy love. In His name Thy children are waiting to show their gratitude by their gifts. First they desire to present themselves and their all, in the name of Him who gave Himself for them on the Cross. Amen.

A Consecration of the Gifts

Many of us think it more fitting to pray after the presentation of the offerings. In plates overflowing with visible tokens of gratitude to God we can find more of holy symbolism than in the same vessels waiting to be filled. Also, a prayer after the offering affords an opportunity to consecrate the gifts, instead of uttering a prayer of dedication; that will come after the sermon. Often we employ these terms interchangeably. More correctly, to "dedicate" means that we give the Lord ourselves and our substance; to "consecrate," that the Lord through His servant blesses the givers and their gifts. Without pausing to discuss semantics, let us assume that every hour of public worship ought to include both elements.

The value of the act in consecrating money depends on the lovingkindness of God, and the faith of His people. The same line of thought applies to the consecration of a seminary graduate who has dedicated himself to the gospel ministry. A few weeks later, in celebrating the Lord's Supper, he will consecrate the bread and the cup, setting them apart for their holy uses. Dedication ought to precede consecration. After any such act, the hearts of the people ought to overflow with gratitude. Hence they may sing the Doxology.

The Doxology usually comes while the appointed officers are bringing forward the assembled gifts. In some churches the Doxology comes after the Prayer of Consecration, a plan that seems more climactic. Whatever the order, the leader sets apart these visible tokens of the people's love to God. For some reason most of the books prepared to help leaders in worship do not excel at this point. One of the best, *Devotional Services*, by John Hunter, includes an offertory prayer worthy of note for simplicity:

Accept, O Lord, these offerings which Thy people make unto Thee, and grant that the cause to which they are devoted may prosper under Thy guidance, to the glory of Thy great name, through Jesus Christ our Lord. Amen.

In a Lutheran church the hour of worship reaches a lofty end by a different route. The offering comes after the sermon, and before the General Prayer, with its thanksgivings. A non-liturgical congregation may follow much the same order. In Newark, New Jersey, the First Presbyterian Church did so for years, and evidently with glad acceptance. This order tends to dignify the people's offerings as a corporate act of sacrifice to God, and to make dominant the spirit of gratitude when they present to Him these visible tokens of their love.

The effect on the minister can be known only to him and to his Lord. In a church with an altar, and with ways of worship different from my own, I once served for two months of summer during five successive years. Among many happy experiences I remember most clearly the singing of the Doxology. After the officers had received the people's gifts, and the minister had blessed them, I took them to the altar. While everyone sang the Doxology, I stood at the altar, holding those gifts, and facing a massive golden cross, in which I could see the reflection of my face. Then I comprehended anew what Arthur J. Gossip had told divinity students about their coming ministry at the Lord's Supper:

Have you realized that one day you will have to stand in Christ's place at His table, [and that you] will be His hand wherewith He gives needy souls that bread that is His body. "Prayer time," says Faber, "is God's punishment time." It is then that our disloyalties come home to roost. I don't know that our sins ever look so ghastly as they do at Christ's table, where we seem to soil the very vessels with our touch, and are afraid that we may block the rush of God's grace to His people.[1]

> When I survey the wondrous cross
>   On which the Prince of glory died,
> My richest gain I count but loss,
>   And pour contempt on all my pride.
>
> .   .   .   .
>
> Were the whole realm of nature mine,
>   That were a present far too small;
> Love so amazing, so divine,
>   Demands my soul, my life, my all.[2]

[1] *In Christ's Stead* (New York: George H. Doran Co., 1925), p. 41.
[2] Isaac Watts.

CHAPTER VI

Praying to
Enforce a Sermon

PRAYERS AND PREACHING BELONG TOGETHER. IN A REGULAR hour of worship either without the other would be incomplete. Opinions differ about the relative importance of the two. Many of us have been trained to believe in the primacy of the pulpit. Gradually we have come to think of the prayers, ideally, as moving on the same high level. All of us ought to agree that a sermon proves most effective, spiritually, when it comes in a framework of corporate devotion. Without thinking of prayers and praises merely as "preliminaries" to preaching, let us consider ways in which prayers may help to enforce a sermon. Surely there ought to be no gap, or break, immediately before a message from God, or immediately after. In cases more than a few, the sermon seems to move on a level different from what comes before, or after. Indeed, the sermon may seem to belong in another realm.

Sentences Before the Sermon

Wise men have striven to bridge the gap before the sermon by having the minister utter a few sentences of prayer, sometimes only one sentence, or phrase. In a Lutheran church the pastor may lead up to the sermon with words like these: "In the name of the Father and the Son and the Holy Spirit."

In the Protestant Episcopal Church a clergyman normally has some kind of vocal prelude to a sermon; it may be an ascription of praise to the Triune God. In bodies less liturgical there may be preceding the sermon a hymn, such as "Spirit of God, Descend Upon My Heart," followed by the Apostles' Creed. Though not a prayer, the Creed affords an opportunity for the people to avow reliance on "the manifold helpfulness of the Triune God."

Before the sermon the order of worship may call for a Prayer of Illumination. At this stage the pastor may repeat every Lord's Day the prayer in Psalm 19:14: "Let the words of my mouth, and the meditation of my heart, be acceptable in thy sight, O Lord, my strength, and my redeemer." While this prayer is full of beauty and uplift, it has to do with private devotions. When used in public, it tends to fix attention on the speaker, at a time when everyone ought to be expecting a message from God, to meet the heart needs of the persons in the House of Prayer.

Why does preaching exist? For the glory of God in Christ, through His blessing on the hearers. As James Denney used to say, "No man can bear witness to Christ and to himself at the same time." In like manner Charles E. Jefferson used to declare that the best preaching voice never is heard, by which he meant that the spokesman for God should call no attention to himself (Cf. Ezek. 33:30-33). In the Prayer for Illumination a minister need not stand under a spotlight. He wishes the illumination to fall on the passage from which he is about to preach, and on the people who await the message from Him who is Light:

Spirit of the Living God, shine upon this open page and bring the truth to light in the face of Jesus Christ our Lord. When we behold Him in this written Word, change us into His likeness, from glory unto glory, for our prayer is in His name. Amen.

The Sermon as an Act of Worship

A Prayer for Illumination leads up naturally to a text. This in turn calls for a sermon distinctly religious from beginning to end. The word "religious" here means something directly related to loving God supremely, loving a neighbor largely, and loving oneself last (Matt. 22:37-39). After a Prayer for Illumination and a text from the Bible, people have a right to expect an introduction and a sermon completely religious. In a university whose debating team won the large majority of its contests the coach insisted on a single rule: As soon as you have stated the question, begin at once to discuss the subject. Put the argument on the highest possible level, and keep it there. A sermon is not a debate, but anyone who speaks to people eager for a message from God ought to begin with truth from God, though never apart from the interests and needs of the hearers.

After listening to countless sermons by able students, a professor used to wonder why they spent so much time getting started. With few exceptions every one of them had a message. At last the professor began to see that the sermon did not come in its rightful place as an act of worship. Before World War II many mature pulpit masters thought it necessary to entertain people for a while before coming to the marrow of the Gospel. These men could write brilliantly about the wisdom of "beginning with the people where they are." Wise counsel, with never an exception! The prophets and the apostles, like their Master, always preached this way. Today in church, after thirty minutes of worship, leading up to a Prayer for Illumination, where ought the people to be, spir-

71

itually? On a mountaintop, in the presence of their Lord, eager for a message that will help to transform their lives.

Sometimes a preacher seems to be afraid of his hearers. He seems to think that they do not wish to hear about God in Christ. At a well-known university chapel on the Lord's Day man after man would lead in uplifting prayers, with equally uplifting music and readings from Holy Scripture. Everything so far would be distinctly religious. Then the sermon would start on a lower level, with the most absorbing human interest, but with seldom a glimpse of God the Father, the Son, the Holy Spirit, or anything else distinctly religious. No one of these men attracted so many hearers, or made so lasting an impression, as a minister who always began to preach with something about God in Christ, with reference to a problem or need in the life of every hearer. From beginning to end this man's sermon never lost sight of the fact that he had been called to preach the sort of Gospel that comes from God and centers in Christ.

Every man who dares to speak for God ought to ponder the words of a well-known university president: "This University leaves its professors free, but it expects every man of them to be grave, reverent, and high-minded." When a man of this type becomes a minister, he can speak for God with an authority not his own. This authority the hearers sense more clearly, and accept more gladly, when he leads up to every sermon with a prayer that takes them into the uplands, with an "air of greater visibility." Ever since World War II many churchgoers have been more concerned about God, and about doing His will, than about anything else on earth. Why should not the preacher "begin with them where they are"?

For some such reasons John Henry Jowett declined nearly every invitation to preach elsewhere than in his pulpit at New

York City. Once in a while he did go elsewhere, and try to preach in a place not intended for the worship of God. Without the sort of "warming up" that comes to a devout man after half an hour of worship he has planned, and then has led, Jowett did not enjoy his customary "liberty of prophesying." He seems to have thought of prayer and preaching as the most important parts of public worship, apart from the Sacraments. Hence he told the students of Yale about the importance of preaching in a framework of prayer:

If men are unmoved by our prayers they are not likely to be profoundly stirred by our preaching. I cannot think that there will ever be more vital power in our sermons than in our intercessions. . . . The climax may come in the sermon: the vital preparations are made in the devotions. I have heard pulpit intercessions so tremendous in their reach, so filled with God, so awe-inspiring, so subduing, so melting, that it was simply impossible that they should be followed by an unimpressive sermon. "The way of the Lord" had been prepared.[1]

The Prayer After the Sermon

The prayer after the sermon usually receives little attention. In many cases it might as well be omitted. Without any conscious preparation, the Lord's interpreter may simply repeat or echo the outline of his sermon, and then ask that the Spirit bless what has been said and done. Suppose that throughout the sermon the Lord's spokesman has been striving to move every hearer to act, in his soul, before he leaves the House of Prayer. Then the few words of prayer after the sermon may be the Lord's way of leading to that decision. Unlike other prayers earlier in the hour, this one may con-

[1] Op. cit., pp. 156-57. Used by permission.

cern the individual hearer. As G. Campbell Morgan once told students at Princeton Seminary, "If you do not move the will of the hearer to act, you have not preached." In cases more than a few, the Lord's representative has not prayed aright after he has preached effectively.

Some guiding purpose ought to dominate a sermon from beginning to end. Whether the message leads the hearer to accept Christ as Saviour and Lord, or to forgive a person who has inflicted deadly wrongs, the prayer after the sermon may well voice such a decision on the part of the man in the pew. This account of the facts differs from the theory that seems to underlie some of the books dealing with prayers for use in public worship. Without thinking about a particular congregation, a special occasion, a specific human need, or any sermon, the editor may write or borrow a prayer that voices general commitment to some cause or other, sometime or other. Fortunately, none of this holds true about the best of these books.

In the New Testament the stress often falls on a Divine-human encounter between the Lord and one person. In the noblest hymns, such as "When I Survey the Wondrous Cross," one person stands in the presence of Christ. In many printed prayers the one person for whom the Redeemer died, the "whosoever" of John 3:16, has dropped out of sight. So has the one person whom the Lord wishes to enlist for Christian service: "If any man will come after me, let him deny himself, and take up his cross, and follow me" (Matt. 16:24). Early in public worship, as we have seen, the stress ought to fall on the congregation as a united family of the redeemed. But toward the end, after the sermon, there may come a decision like that of young Isaiah: "Here am I; send me"

(6:8*b*). Such a decision often comes during the few words of prayer after the message from God.

The decision may assume any one of many forms. For instance, at a large church in the Middle West a visiting professor of church history preached a sermon that showed how much the world overseas needs Christ today. The Chairman of the Board of Trustees had never willingly contributed a cent for any cause, however Christian, beyond our own borders. Because of that message he determined to start at once making up arrears of money for World Missions. That day he handed the professor the largest check he ever had seen, or could hope to see, and all for the Foreign Board. This decision may have come to a head during the brief closing prayer.

In another field the pastor delivers a Sunday morning sermon about the acceptance of Christ as personal Saviour and Lord. Neither in the first half-hour of worship, nor in the main body of the sermon, does he bring out directly the one controlling purpose. He starts with a text from our risen Lord, who is speaking to the worldliest congregation in the New Testament, the church at Laodicea. Once again, note the New Testament stress on a single person, one of many: "Behold, I stand at the door, and knock: if any man hear my voice, and open the door, I will come in to him, and will sup with him, and he with me" (Rev. 3:20).

In keeping with the text, the sermon begins with Christ. The introduction has to do with Holman Hunt's well-known picture "The Light of the World." Then the pastoral evangelist leads up to a truth as welcome as it is unexpected: even in Laodicea, any person may become a Christian. If he opens his heart and receives Jesus Christ as Saviour and Lord, anyone present may become a believer, right here and right now. After such a message, increasingly climactic, how should a minister close? The answer must depend on various factors, not now in view. The pastor at whom we are looking closes in the only way that seems to him feasible.

The last paragraph of the sermon deals with the words "Open the door." Clearly and simply the minister answers the unspoken question of more than one hearer: "Open the door! That sounds beautiful, but in terms of today what does it mean to me?" After his answer the pastor utters a few words of prayer:

O Lord, our God, if there be in Thy House even one heart that is not yet a Christian heart, may He who stands at the door and knocks, with the hand that was pierced on the Cross, come into that heart right now, bringing pardon, cleansing, and peace, with the joy that the world cannot give, or take away. Amen.

CHAPTER VII

Pronouncing the Benediction

In an hour of public worship everything should lead up to the Benediction. If it were missing, or spoken as though inconsequential, the people might feel a sense of loss. In some congregations abroad, if the minister inadvertently fails to perform this accustomed rite, the people remain in their pews until he returns and completes what he has begun and carried through almost to the end. For this line of thought it may at first seem difficult to show a biblical basis, but the conception is in keeping with the spirit of our holy faith as interpreted by the apostles. Paul, however, did not confine his benedictions to the closing parts of his epistles, where most of the biblical benedictions appear.

The Epistle to the Romans has a benediction near the beginning: "Grace to you and peace from God our Father and the Lord Jesus Christ" (1:7). Other Pauline "letters to young churches" start in much the same fashion. Today a minister would do no violence to the facts in the case if he addressed such words to "the saints in Detroit," or to those in Cream Ridge. Sometimes a benediction appears in what seems to us the body of an epistle, as in Rom. 15:13. As for a blessing at the end, everyone has heard the "Apostolic Benediction" repeatedly (II Cor. 13:14). In writing these letters, the Apostle was not laying down laws for newborn churches, but setting up ideals that we still delight to follow, in the spirit of Christian liberty (cf. II Cor. 3:17b).

The Benediction has a long and honorable history. Beginning with Hebrew worship, notably in the synagogue, coming down through the New Testament, and all the later history of the Church, this custom has commended itself to Christian leaders always and everywhere. Without pausing to trace the history in detail, let us consider the nature of the rite, and the importance of making ready for it with care. If at the beginning of public worship the vocal Call to Prayer sets the "tone color" of the service, at the end the Benediction should crown it all with a sense of finality. Such is the ideal. It becomes an actuality whenever the leader knows how to serve as God's agent in bestowing His blessing.

The Meaning of the Benediction

The Benediction may belong with the prayers, but the Benediction is not a prayer. In a public prayer the leader of worship speaks to God; in a Benediction he addresses people. If he uses hands when he calls on a congregation to pray, he has the palms reaching upward. As a rule the minister dispenses with the uplifting of hands in prayer, but he uses them both in a Benediction. He lifts them upward with palms extended toward the people who have bowed down or knelt to receive the mercy that the Lord is about to bestow through His appointed servant. For example, think of a nonbiblical Benediction in one of its varied forms: "Unto God's gracious mercy and protection we commit you; the Lord look upon you with His favor, and fill you with all spiritual benediction and peace; that in this life, and in the world to come, ye may be partakers of eternal grace, through Jesus Christ our Lord."

Other students of prayer look on these facts differently. At present we need think of the Benediction from only one point of view: in this holy act God bestows His heavenly grace on all hearts open to receive it by faith. This interpretation seems to accord with the ideals of Holy Scripture, with the findings of church historians, and with the testimony of Christian experience. In all such matters I claim to be neither inspired nor infallible. Let us assume that the spiritual value depends mainly upon two factors: the mercy of the Giver, and the faith of the receivers.

As for the minister who pronounces the Benediction, he should call no attention to himself. While he should be a holy man of God, set apart for these lofty privileges, the giving and the receiving of God's mercies does not depend upon him, *ex opere operantis*. By this phrase Roman Catholic scholars refer to "the work of the worker," as though he alone held in his hands the key to unlock stores of heavenly treasure. From the Protestant point of view, the minister "pronounces" what God alone can perform.

In public worship a Benediction comes to the congregation as a whole. At a sickbed, as in the act of baptism, the pastor may address only one person: "The Lord bless thee, and keep thee; The Lord make his face shine upon thee, and be gracious unto thee: The Lord lift up his countenance upon thee, and give thee peace" (Num. 6:24-26). As in a marriage ceremony, one need not shy away from the old-fashioned pronoun "thou," or "thee." Everybody present understands that "thou" refers to the one person now before God. In public worship one may employ the same Old Testament words full of beauty, with the word "you" in the plural: "The Lord bless you." In Christian worship one may lovingly add to Num. 6:24-26 these words: "Both now and in the life everlasting, through Jesus Christ our Lord."

The meaning of the rite will become clear and precious to churchgoers if the minister preaches an occasional sermon about one of the Benedictions. For example, he may deal frankly with "The Meaning of a Benediction in Church Today." As the basis of a case study he may single out the most beautiful of all, "The Benediction of Light." Without trying to read into the Book of Numbers all that he has learned through John and Paul, the minister can show that through these words of blessing the Lord communicates the mercies that we Christians associate with the Triune God. In keeping with the topic of the sermon, the stress ought to fall on what a Benediction means in church today. The keeping power of God the Father. The light of God in Jesus Christ. The peace of God through the Holy Spirit. If anyone insists that he cannot see all this in the Old Testament "priestly benediction," he may well ponder the saying of J. M. W. Turner about one of his paintings. Someone told him: "I never saw such a landscape!" The artist replied: "Don't you wish you could?"

The Variety of Benedictions

The Benediction would mean more if the pastor chose it with care, in accord with the latter part of the service. If he has led up to a time "when God's peace guards the door," the Benediction may grow out of the promise in Phil. 4:7: "The peace of God, which passeth all understanding, keep your hearts and minds in the knowledge and love of God, and of his Son Jesus Christ our Lord: and the blessing of God Almighty, the Father, the Son, and the Holy Spirit, be amongst you and remain with you always." Again, after a service of farewell, where everything has centered round the going away of loved ones called to serve God elsewhere, the words of benediction may come from Ignatius. "Fare ye well in God the Father, and in Jesus Christ, our common hope. Amen."

As a rule a minister need not go outside Holy Scripture. In any case, he should plan for variety. If he used the same words of blessing Sunday after Sunday, with no regard to what had come just before, the people might accept the Benediction as a matter of form, which means as little as when one casually says "Good-by," forgetting that the word ought to mean "God be with you." At its best "Good-by" serves as a Mizpah benediction: "The Lord watch between me and thee, when we are absent from one another" (Gen. 31:49). This form of blessing suits better between man and man, or in a social group, than in public worship. But the Bible is replete with other words of blessing that the minister can use in public with little change. Here follows a partial list, to which any student of the Scriptures can add still others:

Num. 6:24-26	Eph. 1:2	I Tim. 1:2b
Rom. 1:7	Eph. 6:23-24	Tit. 1:4b
Rom. 15:13	Phil. 4:23	Heb. 13:20-21
I Cor. 1:3	I Thess. 1:1b	I Pet. 5:10
II Cor. 13:14	II Thess. 2:16-17	II Pet. 1:2
Gal. 1:3-5	II Thess. 3:5	II John 3
Gal. 6:18	II Thess. 3:16	Rev. 1:4b-5a

No one uses all these Bible benedictions. Neither does anyone feel obliged to limit himself to words from the Book. As a rule a man does well to rely mainly on such inspired words as "The Apostolic Benediction," "The Benediction of Light" (Num. 6:24-26), "The Benediction of the Covenant God" (Heb. 13:20-21), and "The Benediction of God's Peace" (based on Phil. 4:7). According to his theological

81

background and beliefs, a man is likely to single out one of these benedictions and use it almost exclusively. Many of us think about religion and life in terms of God's Covenant. So we tend to rely often on the majestic words in Heb. 13:20-21.

In choosing the Benediction, a minister ought to think more about the people than about himself. If he wishes them by faith to receive the blessing that God bestows through His ordained servant, the intermediary should strive to "condition the desired response." One way is to use the bulletin in giving each benediction a name, according to its purpose and character. We may pass by some words of blessing that repeat much the same thing, as Paul often does in his benedictions. In the list above, the stress falls successively on Light—Grace —Peace—Hope—The Triune God—Comfort—Patience— The Covenant—Those Who Suffer—and the Everlasting One. When the people understand any such benediction, and by faith receive the blessing it conveys, they think of it in terms of splendor that comes from God.

For the sake of those who need a benediction, one should be careful not to turn it into a prayer. People also need to join in prayers, but this they have already done. After they have united with the minister in various ways of looking up to God for His manifold blessings, at the end they need a definite act of worship signifying that they are now receiving the mercy they ought to desire at the end of the service. If the minister starts his "benediction" with the word "may," the people do not notice any lack. Many of them never have heard a Bible benediction spoken correctly. But those who have worshiped in other churches may feel that before leaving the House of Prayer they need the crowning touch of God's hand, which waits to fill their hearts with the blessings that the hour of worship has led them to crave.

In all these matters leaders of worship have begun to show more care. When young ministers fall short, they may unintentionally be imitating us older men. Some years ago a faithful servant of God reported that for four decades he had served as Recording Clerk of our chief court, the Presbyterian General Assembly. In all that time, he declared, not one Moderator in ten pronounced a benediction correctly. Man after man concluded an hour of uplifting worship with a brief prayer for God's blessing. If anyone objects that such a prayer can do no harm, that is correct. On the other hand, in an hour of worship each prayer ought to have a purpose and a character different from anything that has gone before. Whatever the form, be sure to make the Benediction a means of blessing, or else quit calling it a benediction. A minister can pray; only God can bless.

A Place for a Doxology

Some of the noblest words of Holy Writ appear in the form of doxologies. Usually we think of a doxology in terms of sacred song, and so we should. But the Scriptures also include doxologies to be spoken. If every minister used such words at times in public worship, there would be less "tameness, lameness, and sameness." In addition to a list of benedictions from the Bible, and from other sources, the leader of worship should have at hand a list of doxologies, written out, nearly all of them from the Bible. Every once in a while in making ready for a particular service he may sense the need for a touch of splendor such as only an inspired doxology can impart.

In the list that follows, the first four doxologies come from the Psalms. Each of them marks the climactic end of a book, for the Hebrew Bible presents the Psalms in five successive parts. The fifth book of Psalms, full of praise, closes with entire songs as doxologies (145-50). The last one the Smith-Goodspeed translation calls "The Closing Doxology." These words from the Psalms we often sing, or hear from the choir. The doxologies in the New Testament, as a rule, consist of exalted rhythmical prose, which calls for utterance at high moments in corporate worship. To the list any student of the Bible can add others:

Ps. 41:13	Rom. 11:33	I Tim. 1:17
Ps. 72:18-19	Rom. 16:25-27	Jude 24-25
Ps. 89:52	II Cor. 1:3-4	Rev. 1:5b-6
Ps. 106:48	Eph. 3:20-21	Rev. 5:12b, 13b

The use of a doxology depends on the leader's desire to express strong emotion. As a rule emotion under control fills too small a place in our public worship. There can be no rules to regulate such uses, because feelings do not follow fixed formulas. For instance, after administering infant baptism, I once blurted out to the people that I wondered why every young man who believed in Christ did not feel an irresistible urge to become a pastor. Would it not have been far more seemly for me to repeat from memory a doxology from the apostle Paul? Again, after a reading about the glory and the mystery of the Resurrection (I Cor. 15:35-58), instead of saying "Thus endeth the morning lesson," one could utter a well-known doxology: "O the depth of the riches both of the wisdom and knowledge of God! how unsearchable are his judgments, and his ways past finding out" (Rom 11:33).

The urge to use a doxology may come while preparing for the end of a service. Very well! Let there be an ascription of praise, but not hasty. After a slight pause, let there also be a benediction. In any such case the minister ought to notify his organist beforehand, lest there be no opportunity for the final benediction. For instance, he has been guiding the people into a sense of the security of heart that comes through trusting in God. At the close he voices their feelings, or what they ought to feel, about the security that reaches out to include both this world and the next. After a doxology of praise, he pronounces the Benediction of the Triune God, who alone can give His redeemed children the Christian kind of security:

Now unto him that is able to keep you from falling, and to present you faultless before the presence of his glory with exceeding joy; to the only wise God our Saviour, be glory and majesty, dominion and power, both now and ever. Amen.

After a pause, and in a quieter tone, the words being familiar: "Grace, mercy, and peace, from God the Father, the Son, and the Spirit, be amongst you, and remain with you, now and forevermore. Amen."

CHAPTER VIII

Leading in
Another Service

By COMMON CONSENT AMONG PROTESTANTS THE MORNING hour of worship has become the main event of the week. In recent years the "eleven o'clock service" has received new and loving attention from the minister and the other persons responsible for public worship. Partly for this reason, church attendance has kept increasing. For all such tokens of God's favor we ought to give thanks. In every congregation the spiritual leaders should also ask Him, and one another, whether the weekly program affords all the opportunities the community needs for public worship. In a neighborhood where Roman Catholics stream into church many times every Sunday morning, and slip in at other hours during the week, what do they think of Protestants who have all sorts of social activities throughout the week, but worship God publicly only once? Do these Protestants put the first thing first?

Nobody believes in needlessly multiplying services. Neither does anyone plead for a larger number so as to compete with Catholics, or carry on the customs of Protestant fathers. Under God, the number and character of the stated services ought to depend on the spiritual needs of the persons the congregation serves. Without argument let us take for granted that the deepest needs of human souls today have to do with worship, and largely with prayer. Why then has many a church kept decreasing the number of opportunities for public worship? Partly because of the difficulty in conducting additional services, and also because they often seem not to have been meeting human needs. In one congregation after another, experience has shown that people come to church at various times if they get what they need, and in an attractive form.

In all such matters one rule holds good. Every hour of public worship ought to have its own objective in terms of human need, and then meet this objective in ways peculiarly its own. Except where increasing numbers call for two or three "identical services," every hour of worship during the week should differ from all the others as much as a well-planned breakfast differs from an orderly lunch, or a satisfying dinner. Whether they know it or not, many people have ceased coming to church more than once a week because they have found the other services much like the one on Sunday morning, and not so well prepared. More serious by far, people who cannot come at eleven o'clock form the habit of not worshiping God publicly every week. So let us think about the prayers in services at other times than eleven o'clock, or ten-thirty.

Early on the Lord's Day

A growing number of churches hold services early on Sunday, perhaps at eight-thirty. Both pastor and people enjoy the hour of worship, and feel sorry if they must give it up during the summer. The service appeals to a limited number of timid folk who shrink from mingling with a large throng; to nurses and others whose work keeps them busy at eleven

87

o'clock; to more than one family that relishes the opportunity to worship in a quiet way, and to burdened souls in quest of hearts' ease. Under the right sort of ministerial leadership the prevailing mood may be that of the disciples gathered early in the morning on the shore of Galilee, to meet with the risen Lord (John 21).

Why should this hour of worship, including the sermon, be identical with the service that comes later? Surely the mood early in the morning ought to differ from that of the more formal service later. Without ever seeming slovenly, the prayers may be more intimate. The spirit of the minister may be that of a pastoral counselor voicing the needs of laymen who may not fill the House of Prayer, but who find there the balm of God for troubled hearts. "Earth has no sorrow that Heaven cannot heal," right here and right now. The healing may come through the minister's prayers, more or less like those at the family altar, where the leader pours out his heart on behalf of those who kneel down together, and of loved ones far away from home, but never far from God. So the prevailing theme at eight-thirty may be the "communion of saints," both on earth and in heaven.

> Though sundered far, by faith [we] meet
> Around one common mercy-seat.
>
> . . . .
>
> And heaven comes down, our souls to greet,
> And glory crowns the mercy-seat.

Late on Sunday Afternoon

A congregation of a different sort responds to a call for vespers. In a suburban community many men and women leave home early and commute to the city every weekday.

Some of them enjoy the restfulness of vespers even more than the inspiration of morning worship, with its appeal to the young in heart. At vespers the mood is that of meditation, amid quiet beauty, with much emphasis on music. People who come to worship at four or five o'clock in the afternoon enjoy a "dim religious light." They welcome a service with a good deal of form, and the leadership of a minister who is more or less a poet. The mood may be that of the two pilgrims who met with the risen Lord while the first Easter Day was drawing to an end (Luke 24:13-35).

As for the prayers, they also may well be meditative, and in the proper sense, restful. At eventide, people enter into the spirit of a collect, a litany, or a bidding prayer—historic forms of prayer that will call for discussion later. People who do not care for such forms do not usually attend vespers. A minister who does not feel at home among these ways of prayer ought not to embark on such a venture. Spurgeon, for instance, excelled in public prayer, but his people would not have felt at home in the sort of service that other persons expect at vespers. Neither would many a devout Lutheran and his flock have felt at home in one of Spurgeon's services after dark. Speaking broadly, a vesper service appeals to people who stress beauty as well as truth, and who have some degree of culture— at least a love for music.

The prayers, too, should have much of beauty. They may breathe the spirit of meditation that fills the devotional classics—another term to which we shall later return. The man who would lead in vespers ought to saturate his soul in the writings of saints who may never have set the world on fire, but who have filled the hearts of readers with love, joy, peace, and many sweet foretastes of heaven's glory. While the forms at vespers differ from those in a Friends' meeting, the spirit of prayers in the late afternoon may be that of Whittier, the Quaker poet, in one of his restful hymns:

> Drop Thy still dews of quietness,
>   Till all our strivings cease;
> Take from our souls the strain and stress,
> And let our ordered lives confess
>   The beauty of Thy peace.

An Hour of Evening Worship

Most churches think of the "second service" in terms of Sunday evening. They regret the passing of the old days when some churches were thronged at night. That was the case in certain areas, but not in most communities during the past sixty years. One by one churches have closed their doors after the morning service, and many pastors have breathed sighs of relief. Here and there a brave minister has shown that people still come to church at night, even in a day when radio and televison provide secular entertainment, much of it froth and drivel. Church leaders seem not to be aware that many intelligent people exposed to such stuff all week would welcome something else, if it were well done, and definitely religious.

An issue of the *Christian Century* (April 17, 1957) contained a leading article about "Vespers in Toronto." Really the service came at night, and achieved "success" worthy of note, despite obstacles common in a church fairly well downtown. The minister and his officers followed a course radically different from that in most churches with Sunday evening services. The Toronto service appealed to people who brought their brains to church, and kept them busy there. The music, evidently, was of a high order. The prayers showed that the leader of this United Church in Canada believed in preparing to pray as well as to preach. Not many pastors could achieve such results, numerically and otherwise, but some of us have never known a community where some church could not hold an evening service of a popular teaching sort.

In a fashion quite different from that in Toronto, and in three fields widely varied, I helped to attract and hold evening congregations of which I never felt ashamed, twelve months in the year. Knowing that unsaved and unchurched folk came to church more on Sunday morning than at night, I did evangelistic work mainly before noon. At night I taught. At the morning hour, except on a special occasion, the service aimed to resemble a symphony, with its varied movements, apparently not closely related. At night in a teaching service everything tended to center around the motif of the hour. If the minister was to preach about "Providence in the Life of a Believer," all the prayers and songs had to do with this personal aspect of Divine Providence.

At the beginning the people might sing "Now Thank We All Our God." Then the prayer would thank God for watching over the friends here present, in all their lives so far, and over every concern dear to their hearts. A later hymn might be "How Firm a Foundation, Ye Saints of the Lord." Another prayer would have to do with the need of God's watchful care just now. The closing hymn might be "Guide Me, O Thou Great Jehovah." Then the prayer would relate to God's tender care in days to come, both in this life and in the next. The idea is that in one sermon the pastor cannot begin to tell all he knows about "Individual Providence." If he lets the entire service—especially the prayers—center around this one motif, he can send every worshiper home with gladness of heart, to come back a week later, when the minister will pray and preach about "The Providence of God in the World About Us."

Worship at Midweek

In many a field the old prayer meeting has passed away, as a victim of senility. Not many people wish to witness a return to the same old lifeless routine. More than a few would welcome "a fireside service," "a pastor's hour," or some other departure from the old rut, provided the newer service lived up to its name. One way is to have half an hour or so of spirited hymns and brief prayers, with another half-hour or less of "animated conversation," about some part of a Bible book that the minister never has had time to interpret from the pulpit. As for the prayers, he leaves them mainly to the people. Gradually he leads them to pray tersely, intelligently, and helpfully. A large order!

The hour of "Bible Reading," not study, may begin with the prayers in the beautiful Third Gospel, the Gospel of Prayer. In passage after passage, each time from a different point of view, the sacred writer brings to view our Lord's teachings and ideals about prayer, most of it in secret. Later the trail may lead to the prayers of Paul, which he reports and echoes, instead of reproducing, word for word. The number of persons in attendance may never reach the proportions of those on the Lord's Day, but in afteryears, when the minister looks back over all the holy hours he has enjoyed in the service of the King, he will give special thanks for these breathing spells in the midst of busy weeks, and for the joys of meeting with the most spiritual of the people. If some of them meanwhile have gone over the river that men call death, in the other world they no doubt find much the same joy and peace that they found in the home church on Wednesday evenings.

In some cities the "Church Night" plan has proved effective. After the day's work, downtown businessmen and women come directly to the church. There they meet with the other members of the family and enjoy an evening meal, well cooked and served hot. The meal is served at cost, and consists of something more appetizing than the conventional meat loaf, with half-baked potatoes. After a bountiful dinner, including a luscious dessert, committees may meet. Many people enjoy getting to know one another better. At eight o'clock all come together for an hour of informal worship, as well prepared and inviting as the earlier repast. "Well prepared" here means variety of fare from week to week, and all of it nourishing. The underlying idea is that people ought to give the Lord's church one night in the midst of every week.

Another plan calls for an "Altar Hour." This could serve as the climactic feature of "Church Night." If so, the stress would fall on the hour of worship, not on what precedes. According to a busy editor who worships at an old downtown church, the "evening Altar Hour has come to be among the most helpful services of the week. The lights are dimmed and the people come to the altar rail as they will, for a time of prayer." Something of the kind has met with much favor on Sunday nights at the large Grace Methodist Church in Atlanta, with Charles L. Allen as pastor.

Here and there experience shows that people respond to any sort of midweek service that meets their spiritual and social needs. The minister ought to remember that "today is not yesterday." Nowhere else in church do people have the same sort of meetings as in former horse-and-buggy times.

The purpose now ought to be much the same as in John Wesley's well-known "class meetings." The reliance must still be on hymns and on prayers, with much use of Scripture, and perhaps an occasional opportunity for testimony. The basic plan for the service ought to vary according to the congregation. So ought the way of conducting it. The Altar Hour would not suit the desires of people with other traditions and ideals. The fact remains that in any church a resourceful minister can have a helpful midweek service. He will do so more surely if he does not stress numbers, but helpfulness. "There is no restraint to the Lord to save by many or by few." (I Sam 14:6c.)

Why does the local church exist? To bring men and women, boys and girls, into right relations with God and with one another, and then train them for service, all through Christ as Saviour and Lord. How can anyone set apart as a minister of the gospel accomplish these lofty ends so surely as by leading well in the public worship of God as often as local needs require? In older days we ministers never found it impossible to prepare for two different services on the Lord's Day and for one in the middle of every week. We know much about the burdens and the distractions of the pastorate today. We also know and admire more than a few ministers who still carry out such a three-point program of public worship, but in ways far different from our own, at least on the surface. Where there is a need, there should be a will to meet this need. "Where there is a will, there is a way." "If any man will do his will, he shall know." (John 7:17a.)

CHAPTER IX

Serving on
a Special Occasion

THE MOST DIFFICULT PUBLIC PRAYERS, AND THE MOST IMPOR-
tant, may have to do with special occasions. As here employed,
the term includes all sorts of services more or less unlike "out-
ward and ordinary means of grace" on the Lord's Day. Sometimes it seems that special services outnumber regular ones.
Tactfully a minister can lead to a decrease in the number of
semi-secular occasions in church. On the contrary, he ought to
thank God for any special hour of worship that ministers to
human needs by exalting the Father, the Son, the Holy Spirit,
or "the great One in Three."

Praying in a Sacramental Hour

Let us begin with Baptism and the Lord's Supper. Opinions differ about many things relating to these sacraments, or
ordinances. All of us ought to agree that the uplift and helpfulness of any such worship depends largely on the prayers. As
for ways of carrying out the service, a minister does well to
follow the forms of the best churches in his denomination.
These forms ought to give Baptism the place of honor it
holds in the New Testament. According to a leading Episcopal bishop, who glories in celebrating Holy Communion,

the New Testament says even more about Baptism than about the Lord's Supper.

Since Baptism normally occurs only once in a lifetime, the ceremony attending this act of Christian faith ought to seem momentous, not momentary. As with all other matters relating to worship, the reasons lie in theology, which in turn comes from the Bible, in the Old Covenant as well as the New. Here follows a prayer at the Baptism of an adult, prior to his first partaking of Communion:

O Lord and Father of us all, we give Thee thanks and praise for Thy loving-kindness to these Thy servants, to whom Thou givest shelter within the covenant of Thy peace, and whom Thou makest to sit down at Thy Table. We entreat Thee of Thy great mercy to perfect in them the good work Thou hast begun; that they, being defended by Thy fatherly hand, and strengthened with power through Thy Spirit in the inward man, may be enabled to keep this covenant without spot, unrebukable, until the day of the appearing of our Lord Jesus Christ. Amen.[1]

At Tremont Temple in Boston a host of us once witnessed a baptismal service for adults. We shall never forget the solemnity of the hour, not least because of prayers by the minister, who relied on words of his own. So did the pastor of the Baptist Temple in Philadelphia at a service I attended, all of it memorable, for the public consecration of infants born to believing parents. When a man of God knows and loves adults whom he has brought to a saving knowledge of Jesus Christ, or when he knows and loves both the parents and the child from a family circle dear to the heart of God, he covets the privilege of voicing the feelings and aspirations of believing

[1] The Book of Common Worship (Philadelphia: Presbyterian Board of Christian Education, 1932).

men and women who stand in the presence of a congregation and confess their faith in Christ, or who renew their profession.

As for the many of us who practice infant baptism with water, we should either engage in the service unashamedly, or else quit baptizing little babies.[2] Without controversy, and with no attack on others who believe only in the baptism of adults, we ought to make every act of infant baptism seem worthy of its high calling. At other times this ideal calls for clear and constructive teaching about the meaning of this holy rite. In the actual "performance," the uplift and the value, under God, depend in no small part upon the prayers. Even if brief they should be memorable. After witnessing infant baptism in churches large and small, friendly observers wonder if such perfunctory performances can ever symbolize the sublimest mysteries of God's covenant promises to believers and to their children. But when a minister loves little babes, and loves the parents, because he loves their Lord, he can lift every such service out of the commonplace and up into the heavenlies where it belongs.

As with adult baptism, the larger the number of infants concerned, the more the pastor's difficulty. Even so, he can utter a closing prayer that embodies two elements usually missing from books of common worship: a petition for everyone present on whom these baptismal vows are resting, and another petition for any person who has not yet been baptized. Without embarking on a sermonic discourse disguised as a prayer, the man with a shepherd heart wishes to include

[2] See Oscar Cullmann, *Baptism in the New Testament*, tr. J. K. S. Reid (London: S.C.M. Press, 1950)—a scholarly defense of infant baptism, in reply to Karl Barth, *The Teaching of the Church Regarding Baptism*, tr. E. A. Payne (S.C.M. Press, 1948).

within the promises of the Covenant God every man or woman, boy or girl, in the House of Prayer, and everyone dear to these hearts. In many a soul the response may be that of thanksgiving; in many another, a longing for a new experience of redeeming grace, or else the return of some erstwhile rapture.

Praying on a Red-Letter Day

For every congregation certain days shine out in the calendar from year to year. They attract larger throngs than other days, and apparently accomplish more of lasting good. The best of them relate directly to climactic stages in the coming of redemption through Christ as the Son of God. Amid all the varied splendor of these triumphant days, one ideal holds true of the minister's prayers. He may choose to roam broadly at other times, but on Christmas, Easter, Pentecost, Trinity Sunday, or any other day of the Christian Year, all the prayers should have to do directly with the one motif. As with the choice of hymns, each prayer should bring to light and exalt some additional phase of the special event. Both the hymns and the prayers ought to lead the people of God up winding ways to a chosen summit from which they can view the wonders of the unseen world.

In addition to a number of these days brought over from the Early Church, and approved by the principles of the Reformation, almost every congregation has still other days that call for special attention. First among them stands Thanksgiving. Like Pentecost, this other celebration does not fall on the Lord's Day. Being Protestant in its American form, without any Jewish tradition or Roman Catholic sanction, the day suffers from neglect. Even so, on an appointed Thursday, or by prayers on the Sunday before Thanksgiving, the minister can do much to restore the pristine splendor. As in dealing with the kindred theme of God's Providence, he can lead, successively, through prayers about the past, the present, and the future—not in one prodigious over-all effort, but with a number of prayers in which lay folk can pour out their hearts to God. No little boy or girl ought ever to forget that on a Lord's Day every year in November the people in church did little else than thank their God. As for other special days, many Protestant churches have gone too far in extending the number. Instead of devoting to this or that worthy cause a whole precious hour of worship, the pastor can briefly include the Boy Scouts, or the Red Cross, in the General Prayer. In the bulletin and otherwise he can encourage the people to give liberally for every cause on which he should invoke the blessing of God. Meanwhile he ought to look on every time of public worship as an opportunity to stress vital aspects of the Kingdom and not to serve as a publicity agent for semisecular benevolent and philanthropic causes.

Praying in Other Pastoral Ministries

As the minister of the church the pastor often conducts funerals. In some communities, as he becomes better known, the number increases. One man had three funerals in a single afternoon. This minister made it a rule never to refuse such an invitation, unless the Lord barred the door. He also resolved that he would never treat such an occasion lightly. Alas, more than once he saw those resolutions wither away. In speaking for God over the mortal remains of a community scoundrel, this pastor sometimes fell back on his *Book of Common Worship*. At the grave his services of farewell may have sounded "noncommittal."

On the contrary, in a downtown area of Birmingham, England, a certain church kept growing in numbers and in spiritual power. One day the verger, a man of discernment, asked the clergyman if he had noticed how the church kept gaining recruits for Christ's army. The minister replied that he had not. Then the custodian of the church edifice explained that after many a funeral the members of a family would begin to attend this place of worship. They enrolled in classes for instruction, and thus came into full-fledged membership, which continued through the years. Why? Not because the minister consciously used hours of sorrow to build up church membership. God forbid! He simply and prayerfully sat where the mourners sat, voiced what they felt but could not utter, and by so doing opened up a spiritual world that they longed to enter—a world where they later found their home in God.

From a funeral a pastor may go to a wedding rehearsal, or a marriage ceremony. There, too, his helpfulness, under God, depends largely on his ability to size up the new situation, and to meet it with wisdom from above. No two weddings ought ever to seem exactly alike. In the ceremony the officiating clergyman should follow the forms of his denomination, unless the bride requests him to "read" the ceremony from the *Book of Common Prayer*. This he should do, willingly, because it is her wedding. If he knows the bride and her beloved, as he should know them before he pronounces on their marriage the blessings of God and the Church, his heart may yearn for an opportunity to voice in prayer certain desires and aspirations different from any in the noblest books of worship.

Such a prayer, spoken from the heart, need not be long. The entire service need not seem long. Sometimes it seems to laymen not long enough. In zeal for "streamlined services," a minister may forget that these two persons now before the Lord need the assurance of God's favor. So do the members of the two family circles, and all the others present. As with a prayer at the baptism of infants, the minister can gather together in a circle of loving devotion all who share the joys of the bridal pair. Not only can he ask the Lord to spare the two each to the other for long, joyous years of love and service in their home; he can also lead many another person, bowed down in God's presence, to renew vows once uttered at the marriage altar.

Sometimes a pastor has to officiate at a wedding where the prayers of the denominational book do not accord with the facts in the case. The two young folk may have "loved not wisely, but too well." Both in private counseling and in the marriage service the man of God should throw open the door of hope that comes through seeking the will of God, it may be after penitential tears, but with a resulting rainbow of heavenly benediction. Generally, in any ceremony that he ought to perform, the pastor by his prayers and otherwise can voice lofty ideals of marriage as the God-given way of establishing a home (Isa. 62:5; Matt. 19:5; Eph. 5:25-27), as the most important place in the world, and as earth's nearest approach to heaven.

Praying at a Secular Occasion

As a minister lives on in a community, he receives an increasing number of invitations to open secular meetings with prayer. At first he may respond with alacrity. Later he may wonder if the Lord wishes him to attend all these meetings. Seldom do they add to his stock of knowledge or lead to any benefit for the home church. Whenever he accepts, he decides to represent the Lord. On any secular occasion, if there is a

101

prayer, it should deal with the purpose of the gathering. It is always proper to give thanks, in so far as one can do it sincerely, without flattery. On a patriotic occasion, for instance, one can briefly thank God for His blessing on the cause that has brought people together.

On a secular occasion it is proper to utter a petition or two for any person or cause to the fore. This may prove difficult. The place and the prevailing mood may not lead a person to feel prayerful. The friends in charge wish the "preacher" to be brief, and to do little but pay his respects to dignitaries who have graced the occasion by their presence. For some such reasons the visiting divine may feel tempted to serve merely as "speaker of the house." In "prayer" he may interest busy men by warning them against contracting stomach ulcers. However ingenious and amusing, such pastoral counsels have little to do with devotion. For instance, take this from a former chaplain of the United States Senate: "We are too Christian really to enjoy sinning, and too fond of sinning really to enjoy Christianity." Or this from the former blind Chaplain William Henry Milburn in the National House of Representatives:

Almighty God, help the people of this country to learn that money gained otherwise than as Thou commandest, by the sweat of the face, as the fair and honest wage of honorable, manly work of brain or hand, is gained by theft, no matter how we name the stealing; that money is never converted into wealth until it ceases to pander to our lusts and lifts us above the level of the animal [and so on through a sermonette in guise of a prayer].

One other sobering fact remains. A minister's prestige at home and elsewhere depends largely on his ability to use God-given powers in meeting a novel situation, and in speaking with distinction on a special occasion. This applies especially to his prayers, brief and uplifting. Such gifts and graces of discernment and utterance enhance a minister's standing among his own people. On the contrary, if he blunders or falls short when the eyes of the community are fixed upon him, the people in the home church may wish they had a minister trained for his office.

At Princeton Seminary, Francis L. Patton used to tell the seniors: "Young gentlemen, there is nothing extemporaneous about a wedding march, or a bride's gown. Let there be nothing extemporaneous about your prayers at the marriage altar." By extemporaneous he meant unpremeditated and unprepared, at least in spirit and in substance. The same counsel holds good about leading in prayer on any special occasion. If a minister has not the time and the patience to make ready, he ought to decline the invitation.

All these principles apply to the Lord's Supper, which appears elsewhere throughout this book. In most churches Holy Communion comes often, even once a week. If the pastor always follows the same majestic forms, the Sacrament may lose its luster. If he seldom voices prayers other than his own, earth's nearest approach to heaven may seem to be blocked. Hence he does well to adopt the noblest forms sanctioned by his denomination, especially the Eucharistic Prayer; and to have a prayer of his own, with a fitting place for the Communion of Saints, here and in heaven.

PART TWO

The Preparation
for Leading

CHAPTER X

Practicing the Presence of God

THE CHARACTER OF A MAN'S GOD OUGHT TO DETERMINE THE nature of his prayers. "Whoever would draw near to God must believe that he exists and that he rewards those who seek him." (Heb. 11:6b R.S.V.) "God is Spirit, and his worshippers must worship him in Spirit and in reality." (John 4: 24 Moffatt.) In terms of today, God is the ideal Person, the One to whom we come for blessings that He alone can bestow. To be worthy of the name, whatever their form, our prayers must be spiritual, and they must be real. For such reasons the devotional utterances of an illiterate exhorter or an untutored Salvation Army lassie may prove more uplifting and helpful than the most precise petitions of an erudite pedagogue who seems not to enjoy a deepening friendship with God.

Sacred learning at its best, however, goes hand in hand with power in prayer. When a saintly scholar leads a group of us into the presence of his Lord, he causes us to feel that God is here, that He knows all about us, and that He loves us, not because we are worthy, but because we belong to Him, being saved by His grace, and called to His service. In the act of prayer, as in all of life, the minister who knows most about Christianity shows in his life that "Man's chief end is to glorify God, and to enjoy Him forever." Without professing to qualify as a scholar or a saint, any minister called of God can cherish the loftiest ideals about prayer. They call for the "holy boldness" of a child who knows the Father well, loves Him much, and longs every day to become more like Him.

A Man Close to His Lord

The man who at times would lead others to God should at all times live close to Him. What this ought to mean for a pastor appears in "the high-priestly prayer" of our Lord (John 17). In the Upper Room, on the night before the Crucifixion, when surrounded by His future Apostles, our Lord opens up His heart and shows what it means to "live, and move and have our being" in God. Among all His petitions for the Church and its ministers, these two may stand out: "Sanctify them through thy truth; thy word is truth"; "For their sakes I sanctify myself" (17:17, 19a). In as far as it relates to Christ, this word "sanctify" does not mean to "make holy," but to "consecrate." As it relates to a minister, the term may mean, in paraphrase, "to make the most of oneself."

For the sake of his Lord, and the people whom he serves, every pastor should make the most of all his God-given powers. According to a well-known description, preaching means "truth through personality," for the sake of meeting human needs. If so, prayer ought to mean God-inspired emotion through the same chosen personality, who voices human needs, especially those arising from sin. Under God, the value of a man's public prayers depends largely on the size and caliber of his personality. This in turn, according to a beautiful psalm, means all that is in a man, both in soul and in body: "Bless the Lord, O my soul: and all that is within me, bless his holy name" (103:1).

Fortunately, his daily routine affords a pastor countless opportunities to make the most of himself by keeping close to his Lord. During long morning hours set apart for study in the spirit of prayer, he can keep feeding his soul with "the bread [of God] which cometh down from heaven," through the Book. At other times when he mingles with people as their God-sent interpreter and counselor, he should still keep close to the Lord. He ought to make constant use of the Bible, in the spirit of prayer. So when he takes part in meetings, he should employ all that he has learned in the study, and through mingling with people. In short, if the health of a good man's soul depends on spiritual food, fresh air, and exercise, the work of a pastor affords all of this day after day.

The unifying power of the most varied pastoral ministry comes through the habit of keeping close to the Lord in the spirit of prayer, and relying upon the Holy Spirit at every turn in the road. Unfortunately, the phrase about practicing the presence of God nearly always suggests the spirit of a cloister, and not ministry among the crowd. Really the phrase should suggest carrying into service amid the crowd the spirit renewed and strengthened in a quiet place with God. This we learn from the record about the Transfiguration of our Lord (Matt. 17:1-21). Also after the Resurrection, when He promised to be with the disciples all their days, He was referring to ministerial services out among men (Matt. 28:18-20).

A Minister on His Knees

"I will place no value on anything I have or may possess, except in relation to the Kingdom of Christ. . . . I will try and remember always to approach God in secret with as much reverence in speech, posture, and behavior as in public." [1] These two resolutions belong together. They come from David Livingstone when he was forty years of age. In his daily walk with childlike people he kept practicing the presence of God. While pressing on through dismal swamps, where danger lurked at every turn, he sang softly to himself the Latin form of the hymn:

> Jesus, the very thought of Thee
> With sweetness fills my breast.

Day by day he "nightly pitched his moving tent a day's march nearer home." At last, when sixty years of age, he came to the end of his earthly pilgrimage. At four o'clock one morning his native attendants stole into the tent of their leader and hero. They tried not to disturb the slumbers of their friend, sick unto death. They found that he had fallen asleep, by the bedside on his knees, no doubt while interceding with God for the Dark Continent where daily he had practiced the presence of God.

Every minister ought to get down on his knees before God, morning by morning, and night after night. Through the hours between, he should "pray without ceasing." This means living in the spirit of prayer. It also means referring everything, often consciously and verbally, to Him "whose service is perfect freedom." Such a habit may call for what the fathers knew as "ejaculatory prayer." They meant that, whatever the place or the need, the Lord waits to hear the cry or the whisper of His servant. Today the term "ejacula-

[1] William Garden Blaikie, *The Personal Life of David Livingstone* (New York: Laymen's Missionary Movement, 1880), p. 155.

tory" suggests something abrupt and impulsive, like the wail of a child awaking from a dreadful dream. Would it not serve better to think of a childlike whisper, with the glad assurance that the Father hears?

For all the saints of God in other days we give hearty thanks. Still their ways were not our ways. They used to hold up as an ideal spending an entire night in a vigil, alone with God. Three ministers once did something of the sort at Oklahoma City, but they banded together. All night they waited on God for His blessing on the work of their churches. From this time onward everyone could see that the climate of the churches had changed, and all for the better. For such times of continued intercession every man of God should hold himself ready, if the Spirit moves. In many cases He does not. Late in life, busy to the very end, Robert E. Speer told a group of us that he had often wondered at earlier saints who could pray all night, but that he himself did not seem to have been built that way. To those who knew him best, he gave the impression of walking with God all day, and of talking with Him many times. He did not need to forego the sleep that would help to fit him, physically and emotionally, for the tasks of the coming day.

On the other hand, Robert E. Speer firmly believed in a minister's setting apart a time and a place for private devotions every day. Speaking as he did in all sorts of assemblies, devoting untold hours to the work of committees, he knew all about the danger of becoming religiously mechanized, if not spiritually "committeed to death."

There have been men in the ranks of the Christian ministry who began Christ's service with high hope and true devotion. Their opening years were full of promise; but they spent themselves in the service of committees. They rushed about from conference to conference. They were never at ease unless they were addressing some meeting, promoting some scheme, absorbed and excited in some noisy philanthropy. The results of such a course of life are always disastrous and sometimes tragic.[2]

An Hour with the Bible

It is not enough for a pastor to have a time and a place for his daily devotions. He ought also to have a self-made procedure. The plan should vary with each minister, but experience shows that everyone does well to rely on two constants: Bible reading and personal prayer. This does not call for a long stretch of one and then a long spell of the other. Private devotions ought to consist in more give and take between two persons who have known and loved each other through the years, though never as equals. First one may ask the Lord to bless what the Book waits to reveal. Then one may read along until a truth calls for light from above, or a duty needs to become clear. So the reading and the prayer may continue. If unhurried, such an hour sets the "tone color" for the day, and sets it in the light of God.

The purpose of the reading is devotional, not didactic. One pastor set up in the study a motto: "No hunting allowed!" This kept reminding him not to look for juicy texts, or telling illustrations, but simply to feast his soul on food that angels stood ready to serve the chosen friend of the King. A man does well to single out a book of the Bible, according to the season of the year, and then live with this book until he knows it better, and loves it more, than almost any other in the Sacred Canon. During a vacation of two months a pastor re-

[2] William M. Clow, *The Secret of the Lord* (Grand Rapids: Baker Book House, 1955), p. 221.

112

solved to read Ephesians through at the beginning of every day. He took no written notes, and mentally prepared no sermons. Daily he read the letter as a whole and by paragraphs, interspersing the reading with prayers. Gradually he sensed that his inner self was being filled to overflowing with water from the hills of God.

The next course of reading may be from an Old Testament Book of narrative, such as Kings, or from a difficult prophecy, such as Jeremiah. In each case one reads differently, according to the purpose and character of the book. Without changing the place of prayer into a cell for study, one can reach out for aid on any passage that seems elusive. Even in private devotions, the Bible helps only when one comprehends it. The effect is not magical. "He that received seed into the good ground is he that heareth the word, and understandeth it; which also beareth fruit." (Matt. 13:23.) The fruit will appear later when the man of God leads in public prayer. If he tried to conduct public devotions without much private use of the Bible, his prayers might seem ethereal. If he persisted in Bible study apart from prayer, his leadership in worship might become biblically informative, but not spiritually uplifting.

Another plan calls for months of devotional reading in *The Prayers of the Bible*. Under this title John Edgar McFadyen deals with them all, except the Psalms. Every lover of the Psalms knows that many of them consist of prayers, some about one person and others concerning a throng or a multitude. One minister found more than sixty of these prayer psalms. In the reading a person does well to take up one psalm at a time. If it is long, he may deal with it only in part. In case of a snag he should reach for a commentary, but not often. Simply by reading the psalm as a whole, and by stop-

113

ping to meditate over each part, one can gain a new sense of God's majesty, and of His nearness; also sympathy for needy souls, and assurance that He stands by to do for them far more than anyone can ask or dream. For instance, take two refrains, each of which rings out four times in Ps. 107, which Alexander Duff, the missionary to India, once used to voice the thanksgivings of survivors from a storm at sea, after their ship had gone to pieces on the rocks:

> They that go down to the sea in ships, that do business in great waters; These see the works of the Lord, and his wonders in the deep. . . . They reel to and fro, and stagger like a drunken man, and are at their wit's end.
>
> Refrain: Then they cry unto the Lord in their trouble, and he bringeth them out of their distresses. . . .
> Refrain: Oh that men would praise the Lord for his goodness, and for his wonderful works to the children of men!
> (Vss. 23-24, 27c, 28, 31.)

Someone may ask: "How can I get an hour for devotions every day in the week?" The answer is simple: "Take it!" Or rather, give it to God, as a willing sacrifice. In the same spirit the minister urges people to give Him at least a tithe of their money, plus freewill offerings. The pastor himself can dedicate to God what seems to him far more precious than money; that is, time. With all our modern short cuts and inventions, it still takes time to be holy. Experience has shown, however, that when a person gives to the Lord gladly, either of time or money, or both, nine tenths will go as far as ten tenths without God's approval. Better still, the nine tenths will all go in the right direction, whether Godward or manward. Surely a minister's time, all of it, belongs to God.

A Life on an Upper Level

Now let us follow the minister out of the study. At noon he goes to a happy manse. There, and elsewhere among men and women, he shows what it means to live as a Christian in this year of our Lord. According to Francis of Assisi, as well as Phillips Brooks, a minister can do good for his Lord simply by walking down the street, or along a country lane. "[His] delights [are] with the sons of men." When he enters a hospital ward to see a member of his church, the pastor can make other patients feel that

> The healing of His seamless dress
> Is by our beds of pain.

Often a pastor must go from place to place quickly and by car. Still he can act as a good Samaritan, not like the priest and the Levite in the Master's parable. Concerning a village pastor of the sort in view, Oliver Goldsmith once wrote: "Allur'd to brighter worlds, [he] led the way."

What has all of this to do with being ready to lead in public prayer on the Lord's Day? Much in every respect! Whether he knows it or not, a pastor is under surveillance every time he appears among men. At first he may resent the fact, but later he discovers that these everyday contacts provide countless opportunities for letting the light of God's presence shine into dark corners of men's lives. Once in Baltimore Maltbie D. Babcock took part in a banquet where some of the men cared little about the church or the clergy. One of them offered the dominie a cigar. Babcock thanked him, but explained that any minute he might be called to a hospital, and that he wished never to enter a sickroom with an odor that would interfere with his ministry there in the name of his Lord.

In our day, sick women may be less sensitive to such things. Still Babcock's underlying principle holds true. As a community representative of Jesus Christ, this minister planned never to attend a gathering, or to take part in anything there, from which he could not go at once to the bedside of a dying saint or sinner. Socially he never acted as a kill joy. His presence cast no damper over a spirit of merriment. Courteously and tactfully he let men know that he stood for God and for goodness. Consequently, he became a power for the Kingdom, both in that city and far beyond. If anyone ever asked why, the answer of his friends and admirers had to do with his personality. That in turn belonged to God. Hence Babcock could sing:

> This is my Father's world,
> O! let me ne'er forget
> That though the wrong seems oft so strong,
> God is the Ruler yet.
> This is my Father's world:
> The battle is not done;
> Jesus who died shall be satisfied,
> And earth and heaven be one.[3]

---

[3] Maltbie D. Babcock, "This Is My Father's World" (New York: Charles Scribner's Sons).

CHAPTER XI

Reading Literature
of the Heart

THE WAY A MAN LEADS IN PUBLIC PRAYER ON THE LORD'S DAY
depends in part on what he has been reading throughout the
week. In addition to the Bible, especially parts full of sanctified feeling, he ought to read other religious literature that
appeals to the heart. Literature here means writing that con-
tinues to live after the conditions that produced it have passed
away. Religious literature of the heart obviously refers to
books that move the soul Godward, instead of merely im-
parting knowledge about things sacred. Within these limits,
which are broad, any minister can select and learn to love
works full of beauty, which the Church will never permit to
die. About these matters let us hear from James Oswald
Dykes, a British theologian who excelled in public prayer, because he had saturated his soul in literature of the heart.

The Classics of Devotion

There is a language of devotion, in which a minister does well
to steep himself. It has been the product of centuries of devout life.
It is not a mosaic of Bible phraseology, but it is modeled on
Scripture examples, and even more on its spirit and tone. It is a
rare essence, distilled from the experience of all saints, fragrant

with their concentrated devoutness. With classic specimens of its literature, which are not numerous, a man would need to be conversant who would catch the mingled dignity and simplicity, gravity and cheerfulness, warmth and chaste reserve, which befit Christian piety at its best.[1]

A list of representative devotional works appears at the end of the present volume. The easiest way to become familiar with the field in general is to read the biographies, or autobiographies, of men who have excelled in things of the heart. At the beginning such a list may include John Bunyan's *Grace Abounding to the Chief of Sinners,* the *Autobiography* of Richard Baxter, and the *Apologie pro Vita Sua* of John Henry Newman. Among books more recent, *Bill Borden of Yale* by Mary Geraldine Taylor, the *Life and Letters of Phillips Brooks* by A. V. G. Allen, *The Life of Henry Drummond* by George Adam Smith, and *John Henry Jowett* by Arthur Porritt. Also, more at random, *The Table Talk of Martin Luther,* translated by William Hazlitt; *The Heart of John Wesley's Journal* by Hugh Price Hughes and others; and *Alexander Whyte* by George F. Barbour.

These books, and many others like them, constitute light reading. They fit into hours at night when a minister needs to relax before he can sleep. They bring him into fellowship with all sorts of men whom the Lord has blessed. As opportunity offers, the list should reach out to include saints before the Reformation. Everybody knows about the *Confessions* of Augustine at Hippo, but not many have read the life of Chrysostom, by W. R. W. Stephens, or of Bernard at Clairvaux by Richard S. Storrs. Such reading will mean all the

[1] *The Christian Minister and His Duties* (Edinburgh: T. & T. Clark, 1908), p. 142.

more if a person marks any book he owns, and keeps notes about one borrowed from a library. On a blank card he can jot down the page number of any item he wishes to copy and preserve for future reference. Happy the man whose storehouse abounds with treasures drawn from his reading of biography! As Sir William Osler says about physicians, the ministry consists of prudent men who take notes and file them with care, and others who mentally live from hand to mouth.

The books known as devotional classics constitute a select library unlike any other. They come from men and women more or less mystical, in the Christian sense of the elusive term. From this point of view, both John and Paul excelled as mystics. So did Mary, the sister of Martha. Sometimes, as sons of practical Martha, an admirable woman whom the Lord Jesus loved, we find it hard to follow the devotional writings of Christian mystics. If we persevere, we may begin to understand the saying of William R. Inge: "The typical mystical experience is just prayer. Anyone who has prayed, and felt that his prayers are heard, knows what mysticism means." [2] Speaking broadly, almost every man who excels in public prayer knows and loves more than a few devotional classics. Among them every minister should have his favorites, chosen with care, and loved to the height.

Love for Books of Poetry

So have the foremost leaders in public prayer been lovers of poetry. According to Frederick W. Robertson of Brighton, a man's choice of a favorite poet serves as a "Nilometer of his soul." In olden days, before men began to control the waters of the Nile with huge dams, the river overflowed, and men

[2] *Christian Mysticism* (New York: Meridian Books, Inc., 1956).

could estimate the size of the coming harvest by watching the height of the rising waters at seedtime. So do all a man's later prayers show the influence of his mastering the *Divine Comedy* by Dante, perhaps in a translation by Charles Eliot Norton; *Paradise Lost* by John Milton; and the *Poems* of Robert Browning. One finds the verses of Alfred Tennyson or William Wordsworth easier to understand, the latter preferably in such an anthology as the small Golden Treasury edition.

As for modern poets well worth knowing, they include Emily Dickinson, Edwin Arlington Robinson, Robert Frost, Alice Meynell, Edna St. Vincent Millay, Stephen Vincent Benét, W. H. Auden, and T. S. Eliot. Not all of these are distinctly religious, but such a long poem as *The Waste Land* by T. S. Eliot shows that recent verse has a message for today. More books of poetry are being bought and read now than ever before in our country. Not all of them hail from Eddie Guest and other rhymsters. When lovers of poetry come to church, they rejoice to find there a pastor who has the heart of a poet.

A wise minister seldom quotes from poets when he preaches, and almost never when he prays. But in three minutes of public utterance he shows whether or not he has lately read anything more uplifting than the daily newspaper and the *Saturday Evening Post*. If in youth he has learned to enjoy the fellowship of men and women who show mastery over words, and if he has continued to read poetry, he can keep drawing words from a "well of English undefiled." The contrast between a person who sees what poets see, and one who does not see at all, appears in lines from Edna St. Vincent Millay:

The world stands out on either side
No wider than the heart is wide;
Above the world is stretched the sky,—
No higher than the soul is high.
The heart can push the sea and land
Farther away on either hand;
The soul can split the sky in two,
And let the face of God shine through.
But East and West will pinch the heart
That cannot keep them pushed apart;
And he whose soul is flat—the sky
Will cave in on him by and by.[3]

A pastor ought also to love his church hymnal. Second only to the Bible, he should know the hymnal better than any other book. When Phillips Brooks first went to the seminary, he could stand up and sing from memory two hundred hymns of the church, with not a flabby song in the list. Later he could write "O Little Town of Bethlehem." Not many pastors write hymns, but anyone can learn to love them. A minister does well to own books of praise from other branches of the Church. Here again, he need not show mastery by quoting often when he preaches or prays, but he can speak out of a heart that loves the songs of Zion. In hours of personal need he can find solace by singing to himself such words as those of Joachim Neander in a German chorale, "Praise to the Lord, the Almighty, the King of creation":

> Hast thou not seen
> How thy desires e'er have been
> Granted in what He ordaineth?

[3] From *Renascence and Other Poems*. Harper & Brothers. Copyright © 1912, 1940 by Edna St. Vincent Millay.

Why not quote snatches of poetry and hymns when one prays? Partly because not one man in ten can intersperse prayers with snatches of verse and song without calling attention to what he is doing. If he does such things adroitly, he may become known for the literary excellence of his prayers. If his own spoken words do not move on the same worthy level, he may call attention to his wide and accurate knowledge of standard hymns. Among prayers by the masters it would be difficult to find one that consists of a mosaic, made from Bible verses and snatches of poetry. Except from the hands of a master artist, a mosaic may resemble the pattern of a patchwork quilt, notable chiefly for its oddity. Elsewhere patches have their place, but in a prayer they reveal ill-concealed poverty of Christian thought and feeling.

Prayers from Other Days

The literature of the heart also includes prayers from days bygone. Many of these prayers a pastor ought to know. Unless he has access to the literature of the Greek Orthodox Church, he may begin with the Roman Missal. In the Latin form it has a sonorous quality that some translations carry over partly into English. The missal contains "all that is said or sung at Mass during the entire year." These forms have influenced ways of worship among other bodies, notably the Lutheran and the Episcopalian. To a less degree the Roman rites have indirectly influenced books of common worship recommended for optional use in other Protestant denominations, each of which has tried to exclude anything not in keeping with the Scriptures, as interpreted by the Reformers.

Gradually a minister can secure a number of prayer books showing the ways of worship in bodies different from his own. From these books he can learn much about what to do, and how to do it well. As for books of prayers compiled by other men, one volume ought to be enough, preferably the one by M. P. Noyes, *Prayers for Services*. So may a pastor have one or two anthologies of poetry, such as the small *Golden Treasury of Songs and Lyrics*, Vol. I, by Francis Palgrave, and *Masterpieces of Religious Verse*, edited by James Dalton Morrison. In times of need, such a work may help a man "prime the pump." In general, a minister does better to rely upon the sources from which editors collect prayers and poems.

Now we come to a question that perplexes many a pastor, needlessly. In a church without prescribed forms of worship, how far can a minister go in using prayers written by other men? Really, there is no barrier, or question about plagiarism. However, if anyone feels sensitive about what people locally may think, he can adopt a homemade rule: "Read from the pulpit notebook any words of prayer from another source; and say with eyes shut anything of your own." Another self-made rule seems more to the point: "When a man borrows a prayer full of golden beauty, he should not mix it with clay from his own garden." Why borrow at all unless one gets something much better than anything of his own?

Within these limits, a minister does well to follow the best traditions of his denomination and of his local church. Among Presbyterians, some pastors follow Calvin, Knox and the majority of our ministers in Scotland today. This tradition calls for dignified ways of worship, and permits the use of prayers from the treasuries of the Church at Large. Here in the States, various Presbyterian congregations follow Puritan traditions almost the reverse. In other denominations, "non-liturgical," much the same attitudes prevail. So it seems that the wisdom of borrowing prayers depends in part on the local situation. In nine cases out of ten, perhaps, a minister need not hesitate. In the tenth church, he ought to use Christian liberty with discretion. In any such dilemma, another homely rule may help: "When in doubt, don't!"

Amid all the present confusion in certain quarters, one general consideration should give practical help. In almost every local church the early part of public worship lends itself at times to the use of historic prayers. In a regular hour of worship other parts may call for comparative freedom from such forms. Except for changes due to passing seasons of the year, the prayers of Adoration and Confession need not vary much from week to week. If a minister ever has difficulty in expressing these emotions aright, he should feel free to employ prayers borrowed from other men. In the parts of the service where he directly voices the needs and aspirations of the people in church, he should know and love them well enough to utter prayers of his own.

On a special day of much consequence the whole situation may be different. If the Boy Scouts attend in a body, their presence need cause no special change in the regular service. But if once in a lifetime a congregation dedicates a new church edifice, the occasion calls for memorable forms of worship. In order to prepare the sort of program that the people have a right to expect, the minister needs a working knowledge of historic forms. As we sing in the *Te Deum*, these treasuries of devotion belong to "the holy Church throughout all the world." On a high day in the history of a local church the pastor should know how to lead the people in worship, rich, full, and uplifting. Thus any congregation can begin to "possess its possessions."

CHAPTER XII

Knowing Historic Forms of Prayer

EVERY MINISTER SHOULD KNOW HISTORIC FORMS OF PRAYER IN use by other Protestant churches. Ideally, these forms ascribe glory to the Triune God. They also lend variety to public prayers that might otherwise seem like ministerial soliloquies. As for the wisdom of gradually introducing historic forms into the worship of the home church, that depends on factors not now before us. In any congregation not yet familiar with such ways of worship, the people ought to approach such a new experience with pleasant anticipation, and afterwards recall it with distinct satisfaction. Otherwise, some of them might feel that they had "offered strange fire before the Lord."

Names of Historic Prayers

Descriptive names that come down through history have a way of changing their meaning. The statements that follow relate only to worship among Protestants, and not to all of them. For example, the word "suffrages" may describe a formal responsive prayer, or else a formal way of introducing a prayer. First the minister says, or sings, a brief "versicle," such as the one below, and the people make an equally brief "response." Worthy examples appear in a book by John Hunter, *Devotional Services for Public Worship*. If the suffrages lead up to a prayer of a different sort, they usually include not more than two or three pairs of versicles and responses. Indeed, there may be only a single pair. At another time the suffrages may come at the end of a prayer, but such a usage is not common. In all these matters there seems to be only one rule: Let the people have a part in this act of public worship. For example, these suffrages may lead up to the General Prayer.

> *Minister:* O Lord, show thy mercy upon us.
> *Answer:* And grant us thy salvation.
> *Minister:* O God, make clean our hearts within us.
> *Answer:* And take not thy Holy Spirit from us.

The word "collect" has many uses. Here it means "one complete sentence, softened by feeling, expressing one thought, and enriching that thought so delicately that a word misplaced may destroy its beauty." A collect needs rhythm, conciseness, and a sense of finality. By brevity and vigor it should catch and hold attention, as well as enlist the co-operation of the people. It is usually spoken by the minister alone. He may use only one collect at a time. Less often there may be a series, each of which calls for *Amen* by the people, as in New Testament times (I Cor. 14:16). A single collect, which may be read, serves admirably as an Invocation. For instance, take this one ascribed to Chrysostom:

Almighty God, who hast given us grace at this time with one accord to make our common supplications unto thee; and dost promise that when two or three are gathered together in thy Name thou wilt grant their requests; Fulfil now, O Lord, the desires and petitions of thy servants, as may be most expedient for them; grant-

126

ing us in this world knowledge of thy truth, and in the world to come life everlasting. [Through Jesus Christ, our Lord.] Amen.

These ideas about collects come chiefly from Percy Dearmer.[1] He calls attention to the fivefold structure of a collect, a form as fixed in rhythmical prose as a sonnet with its fourteen metrical verses, or lines. Only a master of words, with the soul of a poet, can compose a worthy collect, but anyone can admire its artistry, and learn from its form. First there is a brief invocation, usually to God the Father. Then follows a relative clause, which provides a basis for the coming request. Third comes the petition, which relates to a single desired blessing. Fourth is a statement of purpose, showing the spiritual end in view. Last of all, the conclusion, or doxology, provides the climactic touch. Alas, such a description runs longer than many a collect, and lacks its poetic luster.

The Facts About a Litany

The word "litany" also has various uses. Here it means a form of congregational prayer in which the leader voices a series of supplications, after each of which the people make a brief response. The form of the response, word for word, the leader tells the people before he starts to pray. A litany may include a series of confessions, of thanksgivings, or of petitions, but with only one of these in any prayer. Such a litany lends itself admirably to the needs of a special occasion, where the leader wishes to voice desires for God's blessing on a certain cause, or on certain persons. These ideas come largely from Evelyn Underhill.[2] Writing as an Anglo-Cath-

[1] See "The Art of Making Collects," *The Art of Public Worship* (Milwaukee: Morehouse Publishing Co., 1919).
[2] See *Youth in Action* (London: S.P.C.K., 1936), pp. 32, 33.

olic, she says to keep away from vast, abstract subjects, and close to concrete realities and needs, even including individual cases. She also says to keep the responses simple, each time with a brief sentence, familiar to everyone. In general, something like this: "Lord, hear our prayer." After a litany of penitence: "Lord, have mercy upon us."

A variant of the litany has become known as "the bidding prayer." It consists in a number of calls to prayer, voiced by the leader. After each call he leaves a time for silent meditation. Miss Underhill speaks in terms of silence for two minutes each time. Others of us would prefer thirty seconds. Usually the leader allows no more time than for a breath or two. The plan works better, as a rule, with young folk in a gathering of their own than in a group with mature persons who never have learned how to worship God this way. Worse still, some of them may not feel willing to learn. Even so, every minister should know how to make ready for a bidding prayer, and have wisdom to use one only when the time seems opportune.

To prepare for the minister's part in a bidding prayer calls for as much ability and work as for a general prayer. First one studies with care the purpose and the character of the occasion. Then one makes a list of suitable biddings, and gradually arranges them in climactic order. Each call one ought to phrase with care, in a form parallel with the other calls, and so simple that the wording will not call attention to itself. The service may begin with a collect, and lead up to still another collect near the end. Then there may be a doxology, spoken or sung, and a benediction. All of this takes less time than one would suppose.

Let us think about a concrete case. A pastor accepts an invitation to lead in ten minutes of devotion with a group of Christian educators who meet to discuss the teaching of the Bible today. Following a hymn, "O Word of God Incarnate," he reads Isa. 55:10-11. Then he uses a collect, which concerns the Bible:

Blessed Lord, who hast caused all holy Scriptures to be written for our learning; grant that we may in such wise hear them, read, mark, learn, and inwardly digest them, that by patience and comfort of thy holy Word, we may embrace, and ever hold fast the blessed hope of everlasting life, which thou hast given us in our Saviour Jesus Christ. Amen.

Then comes what we call a bidding prayer. In it the leader says, "In reverent silence let us now pray for":

The mother who teaches her little child at home (silence)
The Bible school teacher of growing boys and girls (silence)
The adult class teacher of mature students (silence)
The pastor who teaches people from the pulpit (silence)
The person who teaches the Bible in college (silence)
The professor who trains ministers to teach the Bible (silence)
The missionary who teaches the Bible overseas (silence)

O God, who hast made of one blood all nations of men to dwell on the face of the whole earth, and didst send Thy blessed Son to preach peace unto them that are afar off, and unto them that are nigh, grant that all the peoples of the earth may feel after Thee and find Thee, and hasten, O Lord, the fulfillment of Thy promise to pour out Thy Spirit upon all flesh, through Jesus Christ our Lord. Amen.

Then follows without announcement a spoken doxology (Jude 24), with the Benediction of Light (Num. 6:24-26).

The Eucharistic Prayer

Among these historic forms, many of us love most the Eucharistic Prayer. This is the commonly accepted name for the prayer that appears below. It lends itself to the "air of greater visibility" at a climactic stage in the celebration of the Lord's Supper. The Eucharistic Prayer also proves suitable at the consecration of a new church edifice, the ordination of a young minister, the solemnization of a marriage that touches many hearts, or the giving of thanks for the ministry of a saint who has fallen asleep after a life of heroic service for the King.

The Eucharistic Prayer also provides an element of distinction at a service commemorating God's blessing on the nation. In 1935 English-speaking people around the world assembled in vast throngs to give thanks on the twenty-fifth anniversary of the Coronation of King George V. At the chapel of Princeton University, Sir William Temple delivered an address worthy of the occasion, and of that Christian statesman at his best. The hour of rejoicing came to its climax in the Eucharistic Prayer, printed word for word in a folder of such distinction that many of us have preserved it ever since. As at most other times, the Eucharistic Prayer began with the suffrages known as the *Sursum Corda:*

> *Minister:* The Lord be with you.
> *People:*   *And with thy spirit.*
>
> *Minister:* Lift up your hearts.
> *People:*   *We lift them up unto the Lord.*
>
> *Minister:* Let us give thanks unto the Lord our God.
> *People:*   *It is meet and right so to do.*

It is very meet, right, and our bounden duty, that we should at all times give thanks unto Thee, O Lord, our Heavenly Father, for all Thy bounties known and unknown; but chiefly are we bound to praise Thee for Thy great love wherewith Thou hast drawn us to Thyself in Christ and made us to sit in heavenly places with Him, who is our Peace.

Therefore with angels and archangels and all the company of heaven, we laud and magnify Thy glorious Name, evermore praising Thee and saying:

[What follows may be spoken by the minister, or sung by the choir:]

Holy, Holy, Holy, Lord God of Hosts; Heaven and earth are full of the majesty of Thy glory. Hosanna in the highest. Blessed is He that cometh in the Name of the Lord. Hosanna in the highest. Amen.

A Storehouse Full of Treasure

A minister who has access to historic prayers in use among various churches has a storehouse from which he can keep drawing nourishment for his soul. Also, from time to time he can turn to this unfailing source and find needed help for special occasions. He does well to commit to memory the Eucharistic Prayer and an increasing number of collects. Every once in a while he may use in public one of these prayers, full of beauty and uplift. Often when alone he should repeat such words aloud, to enter into their spirit, and to catch their gentle rhythm. By giving thought to such things, and by storing in memory such words of beauty and power, he can gradually learn to speak in prayer with the sort of prose rhythm that always attends the right expression of Christian feeling.

Such a treasure store, even if not in memory, proves doubly helpful in preparing for a special occasion that ought to seem momentous. Such occasions differ widely, but they all have two things in common. They test the ability and the resources of the man who leads in prayer. Also, they call for prayers different from those at regular hours of worship, and even more uplifting. To these red-letter days in the life of the home church and community, the people should look forward with eager anticipation, and look back afterward with delight. In the actual hour of worship they should mount up as on angel wings, and capture the secrets of the stars.

In view of these ideals the home pastor may follow a simple rule: Make a special service memorable by free use of historic forms in prayer. On the contrary, except for collects, refrain from much use of such forms on occasions not special. Special services here mean those that loom large in the history of the local church. As for a day when the Girl Scouts attend in a body, that calls for nothing much in the way of historic forms. But on one of the "high days" in the experience of the home church, even the most nonliturgical lay officer should not object to special ways of offering thanks to God, and of rendering homage to "the crown rights of the Redeemer."

The difference between a momentous special service and a regular hour of worship ought to appear in the church bulletin. For a service of any moment the officers will gladly finance the printing of a folder that contains, word for word, all the unusual prayers and responses in which the minister and the people take part together. In view of special occasions sure to come, he does well to start making a collection of bulletins from churches that do such things superbly. Instead of merely handing out pieces of paper with conventional printed forms, a congregation can dignify a glorious occasion with printed forms that will cheer and bless lovers of the local church, both at home and beyond the seven seas. "The leaves of the trees [shall be] for the healing of the nations." (Rev. 22:2c.)

CHAPTER XIII

Sensing the
Needs of People Now

A MAJOR PORTION OF A PARISH MINISTER'S LIFE AND WORK consists in being a first-rate pastor and personal counselor. Perhaps our discussion of ways to make ready for public prayer ought to have started here. Without accepting all that comes from Barth and Brunner, or Buber and Kierkegaard, we may learn from them the importance of taking human ills seriously. What they call the "existential element" has as much to do with prayer as with preaching or theology. So the discussion from here onward will concern a "people-centered ministry." When a minister prays in church, nothing on the human level ought to bulk so large as what the people here present need right now.

Sympathy with Home People

Fortunately, these concerns refuse to stay on the human level. When a minister sees people in their homes, or confers with them one at a time in a room at the church, he needs to look up for guidance and restraint. Like Lincoln in the White House, the pastor has nowhere else to go. In case after case he cannot even make a correct diagnosis. Somehow human ills do not fit the classifications of books and schools. If a pastor is sensitive to human needs, he soon forms the habit of "the upward look." A wise program of pastoral nurture calls for untold expenditure of time and energy, both of soul and of body. In addition to the good a man does from day to day, the fruitage appears in church when he leads in prayer.

"The [minister] must live with the people if he is to know their problems, and he must live close to God if he is to solve them," says Joseph Fort Newton. Amen! But sometimes we forget that a third element enters into every such equation. As a servant of God and a helper of men, a pastor needs to engage in a people-centered ministry for the good of his own soul. With the soul as with the body, abundance of nourishing food, with little or no exercise, may lead to flabby muscles and a weak heart. For such reasons the man who leaves an all-round pastoral ministry to become a full-time professor finds it hard to keep up his prayer life. On the Lord's Day, when he leads in an hour of worship somewhere, he may preach almost as well as before, but afterwards he may wonder why he has lost the old-time rapture while leading in public prayer. He has not recently enjoyed those former loving contacts with persons in need of what God alone can supply.

Often we ministers have smiled over a medieval word picture showing

> The parish priest
> Of Austerity, [who]
> Climbed up in a high church steeple
> To be nearer God,
> So that he might hand
> His word down to His people.[1]

Alas, we feel more like tears when we think of such a man

[1] Brewer Mattocks, "The Preacher's Mistake."

trying to pray in church, week after week, for people whom he does not know, or want to know. Early in the ministry the right sort of pastor learns to "rejoice with them that do rejoice, and weep with them that weep." "In all their affliction he is afflicted." Originally written about the Suffering Servant of the Lord (Isa. 63:9), these words hold true of every minister who follows in His train.

Of late these matters have been changing for the better. Many factors have united to cause a ministerial rediscovery of the individual and his needs, with much emphasis on pastoral counseling. Naturally a physician of souls deals with only one person at a time. Largely because of this return to New Testament ideals, public prayers have also improved. And yet many a layman who feels loyal to the minister reports privately: "He preaches well, but he is not a good pastor. He does not know his people." Such a layman might also report: "He does not excel in praying for the home folks." Every once in a while such a layman steals away from his world-famous preacher to seek assurance and strength from an unknown pastor who can pray for people in distress, because this unknown man has spent his life ministering to all sorts of suffering persons, one by one.

Any clergyman who does not choose to engage in a "person-to-person ministry" can occupy himself in other forms of useful service. He can also try to justify his refusal to ring doorbells and otherwise seek for a silly sheep that has strayed from the fold. Fortunately, the Man of Galilee never acquired the sort of farsightedness that can sense the needs of the world, but not those of a person near at hand. Today the difficulties of engaging in pastoral work have multiplied. Conditions may call for many changes in method. Meantime these human needs persist. The man who does his full share in helping to meet them locally throughout the week can pray about them profitably on the Lord's Day.

Concern About Distress Elsewhere

The most diligent pastor, alas, may be nothing but a home pastor. If so, his prayers must seem provincial. Apparently he forgets that God loves the world, and that "nothing human is foreign" to a minister who seeks first the Kingdom of God. All week his people read about affairs of moment in the Far East, the Near East, and the Middle East. Often over radio or television they listen to wide-awake commentators telling about persons and events beyond the seven seas. One thing laymen almost never read or hear: a spiritual interpretation of the passing world scene with its kaleidoscopic changes. On the Lord's Day when they come to church and take part in prayers confined to their own community, they may wonder if the Church really cares about conditions in Poland, and if the Gospel has any relevance to the needs of Red China.

Without assuming an air of "superficial omniscience," the pastor needs to know the main currents of thought, feeling, and action among the nations of the earth. When he leads in prayer, as when he chooses hymns, he should know how to voice the aspirations of people who wish their sons and grandsons never to cross the seas for war; fathers and mothers who will take no rest until the children of India have food enough and to spare, with all the other privileges and opportunities that our own boys and girls enjoy as a matter of course. The minister should likewise show concern about the plight of minority groups here in the homeland. As with many such problems he dare not speak with authority about the form of the coming solution, but he should make clear that God still rules, and that He will take no rest until the members of every race on earth have all the rights and privileges that He wishes them and their children to enjoy.

One field the pastor can make peculiarly his own. In the realm of World Missions he should know more, and feel more at home, than anyone else in the congregation. He may not often preach directly about Missions, because such discourses usually fall short of their purpose. But he can know and care enough about the matter to pray about it intelligently and feelingly at every hour of regular morning worship. During a period of three years a pastor new on the field never preached a full-length missionary sermon, and he seldom introduced a Sunday-morning missionary speaker. In that time the congregational giving for Missions overseas quadrupled, partly because his prayers and sermons were saturated with the spirit of making the whole world Christian. When the pastor feels the thrill in the "romance of missions," the people soon begin to be missionary-minded.

A working knowledge of Missions does not come easily, overnight, or in ten weeks. Not only does it call for a working knowledge of the facts about Missions today, especially in one's own denomination; mastery in the field also grows out of reading lives of well-known missionaries. In this field every lover of biography has his favorites. Here follows a list of books that one minister has read with interest during evening hours when he felt too weary for hard intellectual labor. Many of these books have gone out of print, but they are all available at any first-class seminary library:

Life of David Brainerd, Missionary to the Indians by Jonathan Edwards, *Life of William Carey* by George Smith, *Autobiography and Letters of James Chalmers, The Life of Alexander Duff* by George Smith, *Christina Forsyth of Fingoland* by William Pringle Livingstone, *Labrador Doctor* (autobiography of Wilfred Thomason Grenfell), *Sam Higginbottom, Farmer* (autobiography), *Pastor Hsi: One of China's Christians* by Mary Geraldine Taylor, *Life of Adoniram Judson* by Edward Judson, *The Personal Life of David Livingstone* by William Garden Blaikie, *Memoirs of the Life and Correspondence of Robert Morrison* by Mrs. Robert Morrison, *John C. Patteson of Melanesia* by Charlotte M. Yonge, *John G. Paton, Missionary to the New Hebrides* (autobiography), *James Robertson* by Charles W. Gordon, *Albert Schweitzer* by John D. Regester, *Mary Slessor of Calabar, Pioneer Missionary* by William Pringle Livingstone, *Hudson Taylor's Spiritual Secret* by Howard Taylor, *Samuel Hall Young of Alaska, the Mushing Parson* (autobiography).

Like everything else that a minister knows and loves, missionary biography influences his public prayers. He dare not ever employ a prayer to promote Missions. He always speaks to God, not to provide Him with information, or to dictate how He shall govern the world, but to plead for the fulfillment of His promise that the kingdoms of this earth shall become the Kingdom of our Christ (an echo of Rev. 11:15), and that He shall reign forever and ever. This kind of intercession does not consist merely in saying: "Lord, bless China"; "God bless Africa"; or "Look in mercy on the islands of the seas." A minister who knows the facts about Missions, both yesterday and today, would never dream of flying swiftly round the world without stopping to visit any station or meeting any missionary.

In short, before a pastor can make ready to pray in public, he must have a Christian philosophy of life. Does he actually believe that God "holds the world in His hands," and that He cares about the fall of a sparrow? In a world filled with rumors of war, can he in every prayer voice the spirit of Christian optimism? Not unless he holds firmly to the revealed truth about God's Sovereignty. Such a working philosophy enables a minister to pray intelligently about "the world and the individual," both of them dear to the heart of the Eternal. He dare not think that we yet live in "the best of all possible worlds," or that "every day and in every way the world is growing better and better." Still he can pray with a heart full of peace, joy, and hope. Well does he know that the drama of world redemption will issue, not in defeat and confusion, but in triumph and glory.

A Habit of Keeping Notes

Now let us descend to a level where some of us feel more at home. In order to make ready for prayers on the Lord's Day, a minister does well to keep notes throughout the week. He may not deem it prudent to include on Sunday all the items he has jotted down. If some remain over, he can add them to the list for the coming week. In a thin notebook, or on a few cards of stiff paper, he can jot down items of various sorts, mainly three: those relating to the home church and community, others about his own country elsewhere, and some about the world beyond.

The idea is to have at hand salient facts about the experiences and impressions of the past week. Otherwise the representative of God's people may come before the King with much the same thanksgivings, petitions, and intercessions week after week. He need not pray about local persons by name, or serve as a chronicler of current events, whether local or at a distance. Without ceasing to pray Godward, a wide-awake pastor can lead the people every Lord's Day through a land of hills and valleys, which seem to them new and strange, until at last they catch a glimpse of Bunyan's Celestial City.

A suggestion of a different sort comes from George S. Stewart of Edinburgh. His book *The Lower Levels of Prayer* shows that he is at home in private ways of intercession. Elsewhere he advises a busy pastor to look ahead for a month, or a longer period, and draw up a tentative calendar showing which causes to include on successive Sundays. As with the prior suggestion, this plan would work in three concentric circles: the home community, the country elsewhere, and the world beyond. For example, on every Lord's Day a minister does not pray for the men who guard the lives, the health, and the property of the home town. Once in a while he may remember before God the policeman on his beat, the health officer in his rounds, and the fireman at his post.

In March, when sickness abounds, the petitions on a Sunday may include the physician, the surgeon, and the nurse. At another time, the patient who is wasting away with cancer, the person who waits on such a loved one, and the man of science who toils to discover a cure for this scourge. On a Lord's Day before the opening of the public schools the minister who loves boys and girls commits them to the care of their heavenly Father and His servants, the teachers. "They that are the teachers shall shine as the brightness of the firmament; and they that turn many to righteousness as the stars for ever and ever." (Dan. 12:3 A.S.V. margin.)

Any such plan calls for skill and care. A man without common sense and tact might make a personal, factual prayer seem absurd, if not ludicrous. On the other hand, John Watson in Liverpool used to pray for anyone who had "lost the kindly light of reason." According to statisticians, fifty per cent of the hospital rooms in our country are occupied by persons whose maladies concern the mind more than the body. Almost every congregation includes a household from which a member has been taken to the state hospital, apparently for life. And yet the minister may never pray for sick persons except those with bodily ailments, from which the large majority of patients soon recover.

When a man has a shepherd heart, he may find it hard to omit the mention of persons and causes about which he longs to pray in public. If he has at hand some such homemade schedule as Dr. Stewart suggests, or else a few cards on which he has jotted down items culled from the week's experiences and impressions, he can come to Saturday morning ready to single out matters about which he feels sure the Lord wishes him to pray on the morrow in church. Instead of relying on memory, or on "the inspiration of the moment," he has at hand facts, facts, facts, the assembling of which has taken neither time nor effort. Even if he feels jaded, a review of these data should help to revive his fainting spirits, and enable him to make ready for leading others into the uplands of God.

Under the guidance of the Holy Spirit, the value of these data will depend on his giving imagination the right of way. This term, "imagination," employed in many other ways, here means the God-given power that enables a gifted man to put himself in the other person's place, look at his world through his eyes, feel as he ought to feel, and then use heaven-born words in leading above things earthy and up into the radiant light that streams from the face of our crucified and risen Lord.

CHAPTER XIV

Reserving a
Time to Prepare

WE HAVE BEEN ASSUMING THAT THE IMPORTANCE OF MAKING ready for public prayer warrants a minister's setting apart a definite time near the end of every week. We have been thinking about Saturday morning, the earlier the better, so that he may feel refreshed by sleep, and be free from interruptions. Except for an occasional emergency, the work of pastoral ministry and counseling should lie behind his back. Apart from the final stages of making ready to speak in the pulpit, his sermon ought to be ready. So he can prepare for the service as a whole, and then for each successive part, with the main emphasis on the prayers.

First the pastor needs to prepare his own heart. Like the Hebrew priest of old, before a man of God offers sacrifices for others, he should come into the presence of God on his own behalf. Like the Hebrew priest wearing a breastplate bearing the names of the Twelve Tribes, the man with a shepherd heart carries into the Lord's presence the needs and aspirations of people for whom he will pray in church on the morrow. If he is wise, he has learned to "see faces." More than one pastor has formed the habit of stealing into the sanctuary when no one else is there, and of going from pew to pew, praying by name for each person who will worship there.

In some such fashion John Henry Jowett used to prepare his heart for leadership on the morrow. More recently at the City Temple in London, Leslie D. Weatherhead has followed much the same course. After a period of fellowship with living men and women, whom he knows and loves, and of fellowship at times with "the spirits of just men made perfect," a pastor should feel ready for the ordering of his petitions and supplications, according to a simple plan of his own devising. Thus far he has been thinking of this person and of that, with a different little group every week—representing the congregation. When he comes to the work of preparing directly, he makes ready to lead the congregation as a whole.

A Plan for the Entire Service

Before he dares to lead in an hour of formal worship, a minister ought to have a self-made plan for the service as a whole. To the making of this plan he should devote even more attention and care than his wife gives to preparations for an evening dinner with a number of guests invited to honor a distinguished missionary. If a minister forms the habit every week of making such an over-all plan, the work will in time become far less difficult. Still he must watch the season of the year, the time of day, and any special feature, with due regard to the sequence of parts.

Before him lies the order of services. In it appear various items, such as hymns and readings from Holy Scripture. Here and there, not too close together, come acts of prayer, each with a purpose and character all its own, and clearly marked in the bulletin. Following this familiar guide, he can plan so that each prayer will follow naturally after what has gone before, and lead up easily to what will come next. There should be no gap, break, or jar.

Without neglecting any other part of worship, the pastor can make ready so that prayers will mark climactic stages in the upward course of devotion. The first climactic stage in prayer may come during the corporate Confession of Sins. No matter how often one reads the account of young Isaiah's vision, all in terms of worship (Isa. 6:1-8), one should never lose a sense of awe and wonder when one throws oneself on the mercy of God and asks for the pardon of sins, both one's own and those of other people.

A still more climactic experience comes in the Assurance of Pardon with cleansing, and peace. All of these have to do with worship. In Isaiah's vision the coal that symbolized cleansing came from the altar of burnt offering. Today cleansing and peace come through a vision of the Cross and the influence of the Spirit. This feeling of assurance, with the resulting glow, ought to fill and flood the General Prayer, leading up at the close to the simple, soul-satisfying words of the Lord's Prayer. Today the experiences of redeemed persons differ from those of young Isaiah. The fact remains that the Holy Spirit guided him in that hour of soul adventure and discovery, and that he passed through successive stages, each more wondrous than the one before. With some such vision the pastor can make ready for the longest and most important of his public prayers.

The chief climax may come during the Prayer After the Sermon. At this stage, because of all that he has heard and felt in the House of Prayer, the worshiper ought silently to whisper: "Here am I; send me." In a high sense this is for him the one divine event toward which the entire service has been moving. Whether the dominant aim of the hour is soul

145

winning or life building, there should come a moment that certain wise men call "existential." This does not mean that the sermon ought to dominate everything, but that the service as a whole, including the best sermon a man can prepare, should lead everyone present to make a personal decision about the matter now at the fore.

The Preparation of Each Part

Having such a vision of a service with prayers at climactic stages, a minister sets to work. He may use an order different from the one that here follows, but any person trained to lead in worship can make the necessary adjustments. First he may prepare, word for word, the Call to Prayer. He may already know the Bible words by heart. If not, he should commit them to memory, and on the morrow say them, eye to eye, heart to heart. In order to do so with assurance, let him write them out, word for word. Then he can write out the brief Invocation. If he plans to use a collect, he may copy it, in double space, or else insert a card with these stately forms, unchanged. So with words of Confession, which come after a pause for silent prayer. These words, too, may appear in the notebook, without departing from the style of the original, unless a man chooses to write out a prayer of his own. If he works both ways, at different times, he will have variety in the Confessions from week to week.

The same counsel applies to the prayer over the offering, to any other brief words of prayer, such as the few words of soul dedication after the message. "Be not rash with thy mouth, and let not thy heart he hasty to utter any thing before God: for God is in heaven, and thou upon the earth: therefore let thy words be few." (Eccl. 5:2.) At first the writing out of brief prayers may seem like drudgery. If a man

146

keeps his ideals up where they belong, he may never find writing easy. But little by little, then more and more, he will learn how to order his words aright. If at any time his spirit falters, so that words will not come, he can turn to a collect.

As for the General Prayer, or prayers, the suggestion here calls for a careful outline. This, too, ought to appear in the notebook, but only to make sure that one has something worth saying to God, and that it will come in a form easy for laymen and their children to follow. Except when reading a prayer of the ages, without having had time to store it in memory, a man does well to pray with his eyes shut. The fact that he has made a plan should guide in all that he says, just as in delivering a sermon he can speak without notes, and still not depart from the route he mapped out in the study. To this idea of planning a prayer, without writing it out in full, we shall later return. Let us now consider the idea of writing out short prayers.

"The Habit of the Pen"

This phrase about the use of a pen comes from the autobiography of the late Bishop Edwin Holt Hughes. What he says may refer in part to preaching, but he would agree about the application to public prayer. After years spent in the oversight of local pastors, he was asked about the prevailing sin of the ministry. He replied, "Extemporaneousness!" By that he meant, not the utterance of words that well up from the heart at the time of utterance, but the habit of voicing thoughts and feelings on "the spur of the moment," with no prayerful preparation of content. If any reader searches his heart, and mentally reviews his public prayers for the past month, he can make his own word picture of "extemporaneousness." First, listen to the Bishop:

The habit of the pen is not only a taskmaster that commands to industry; it is a guard against carelessness, . . . I have a tremor when I recall how I almost succumbed to extemporaenousness . . . . When we are careless in preparation we are not good men. Extemporaneousness may spell the loss of character. We are followers of One who said, "I must work." [2]

When Bishop Hughes spoke to men on behalf of God, he moved with ease among the mightiest truths of the Kingdom. When he, with eyes closed, appealed to God on behalf of men he spoke with equal assurance and grace. If anyone had asked how he acquired such mastery, he might have replied: "With a great sum obtained I this freedom" (Acts 22:8a). The same held true of Spurgeon. His admirers have sometimes pictured him as a "freeborn" master of moving words; as one who "lisped in numbers, for the numbers came." Spurgeon's Autobiography, in four large volumes, shows that every week he spent all of Monday, and sometimes much of Tuesday, in self-imposed discipline of the pen.

Before Spurgeon let a sermon go round the world in a printed form, he revised it with as much care as Joseph Fort Newton later had to use in writing daily syndicated religious articles that would pass the eye of a secular editor. And yet some admirers thought of Newton as being born with the gift of ready utterance. John Calvin is said always to have written out his public prayers, but not his daily sermons. Much of the same held true about written classroom prayers by the late Dean Edward Increase Bosworth at Oberlin College. So it seems that strong men of various schools, doctrinally, unite with Bishop Hughes in calling for "the habit of

[2] *I Was Made a Minister* (Nashville: Abingdon-Cokesbury Press, 1943), pp. 312-13.

the pen." After the first five or ten years some masters of public prayer cease to write out so much as at the start.

The Element of Time

Someone may ask why the stress falls on writing out short prayers rather than the sermon. The answer is that a man ought to do both. In addition to writing out in full one sermon every week, a pastor may set up the ideal of writing out all the short prayers for morning worship. In addition to the assurance of having something to say, and a clear idea of how to say it, a man who uses his pen for the glory of God and the welfare of people has a homemade way of preventing the sort of wordiness that often comes with increasing years. Perhaps wisely, a present-day congregation expects a minister to keep the morning service within sixty minutes, or thereabouts. If during that time he is to voice the desires and aspirations of people who need God, he dare not waste a single word.

A man does well to keep a file of his written prayers. In one folder he may have Invocations, and in another his own forms of Confession. In case of need, though not often, he can fall back on words of his own that he has used before. So much do some ministers value "the discipline of the pen" that they form the habit of putting on paper some of their private devotions. Samuel Johnson must have done something of the sort, and so did Bishop Lancelot Andrewes. If anyone suffers from wandering thoughts while ostensibly speaking to God, he may try this plan of writing out what he feels to be worthy of telling the Person to whom he pours out his heart.

This chapter may leave the impression that the average minister preaches better than he prays. If any man wonders whether or not this generalization applies to him, let him have a lay friend make a recording of everything spoken in church during the coming month. Then let the minister, alone with his Lord, listen to what he has said to God and to men. If he discovers that his prayers are repetitious, even verbose, let him ask why. If frank with himself, he may acknowledge that he has spent hours in preparing to preach, and only a few minutes in making ready for public prayer. As for the remedy, a man who does not have the gift of "mental composition" ought seriously to consider setting apart on Saturday morning time enough to write out every brief word of devotion, planning with equal care what to say, and how to say it, in his longer prayers. As a consequence, no one of them should ever seem long. Thank God for "the habit of the pen"!

CHAPTER XV

Making a Pattern
for Each Prayer

THE EFFECTIVENESS OF ANY PUBLIC PRAYER DEPENDS PARTLY ON the way it follows a simple pattern. The value, under God, depends far more on the spirit of the leader, and on the substance of his prayer. Anyone could give examples of ministerial saints who voice the noblest desires in ways that people do not follow, and of less godly men who utter less exalted prayers that the same people follow. If one may echo an Irish divine, Archbishop William Magee, three sorts of men lead in public prayer: the one whom the people can follow if they make up their minds; the one whom they cannot follow, however much they so desire; and the one whom they always follow, without conscious effort. The number of ministers in this third class seems to be increasing, but there is room and need for many more. The differences among the three relate in part to literary structure.

The structure of a prayer should call no attention to itself. Like the trellis that supports a vine laden with grapes, the framework of a prayer serves only as a means to an end nobler than itself. Without such an inner support, planned and made for the purpose, a vine would not bring forth luscious grapes, and it would have no beauty that men should desire it. In everything that God has made, He has followed a design in accord with His purpose. So in every prayer that He guides a minister in preparing, God wishes His servant to employ all his powers in adapting human means to heavenly ends. For examples in support of this thesis, let us think of prayers that the Lord has blessed. In all the history of devotion it would be hard to find an effective prayer without a simple pattern.

Examples from Bible Prayers

Every prayer recorded or reported in the Bible follows a pattern. Many of these prayers have to do with one person and his God. Among those that voice a leader's aspirations for a group or a multitude, let us think about the longest (I Kings 8:22-53). Without pausing to consider critical questions, read Solomon's prayer aloud, noting how easy it is to follow, and to recall. Why does the prayer hold attention today, despite the fact that no one now has gone through these experiences, such as famine, which meant everything evil to the Hebrew people? For the present we may think about the answer only in terms of structure, as distinct from literary style, though the two are inseparable.

This prayer follows a simple pattern. The leader begins with a few words of Adoration. Then he utters a brief petition for the ruler of the land, with a short paragraph about the new Temple. The rest of the prayer has to do with vital concerns of the assembled throng: a man who has done his neighbor wrong; people who have met defeat in battle; sufferers from drought, like those in our Texas at times; victims of famine, and of pestilence, which follows drought; a foreigner in the land, one of a "minority group"; an army going to war; and people when they sin against their God.

"Today is not yesterday." No one now would voice these

same desires, in these exact forms. But anyone can see that
the leader has been following a simple pattern of his own de-
signing. Evidently he has "begun with the people where they
are." Instead of merely praying about a building, he has voiced
the desires that should fill the hearts of all the people present.
He has followed an order of dealing with well-known needs,
beginning with what most strongly affects everyone present,
and leading up to what should most deeply concern them
all. From beginning to end the prayer gives a sense of onward
motion. It proves easy to follow because it embodies Hebrew
parallelism, stating similar facts in similar forms. It also sounds
a striking motif, which rings out again and again, to mark the
transitions: "And hear thou in heaven thy dwelling place: and
when thou hearest, forgive."

If the leader spoke deliberately, averaging 130 words a
minute, his prayer would require approximately eight minutes.
Too long, much too long, except on such a memorable occasion, which can come only once in a lifetime, and may not
come at all! On any other occasion a minister can single out
the desires that he ought to express, and in three minutes
voice them in a way that proves effective. For examples of
prayers not lengthy, turn to the New Testament.

Everyone thanks God for the simplicity and the terseness
of the Lord's Prayer. It embodies a careful design, with three
petitions in the first main part, and three others in the second.
They follow the principle of parallelism, but not in a wooden
way. They all look in the same direction, upward. In a so-
called prayer of much the same length, an ordinary man, unprepared, could try to lead in six different directions, having
to do, successively, with the speaker, the hearers, the occasion,
the weather, the theme of the coming sermon, and the presence of God. How can people follow even a brief utterance

by a man who does not know whither he is going, or how he plans to get there?

Let us turn to the "high-priestly prayer" of our Lord. He is with the disciples in the Upper Room on the night before the Cross (John 17). Like the prayers of Paul in Ephesians, which are not for public worship, this one does not show the simplicity of prayers among people in general, but still it illustrates the use of structure. According to Bengel, Christ here prays for Himself, for others near at hand, and for the Church at large. Some of us prefer to think about the first part as concerning "The Glory of God the Father" (vss. 1-5); the second, "The Security of Believers Here at Home" (vss. 6-19); the third, "The Unity of the Church at Large." This unity seems to be that of the Spirit, rather than the body, but this does not directly concern us now. We should rejoice in the spiritual union of all who receive and glory in the ideals of the high-priestly prayer.

If anyone goes further in the analysis, he will find that each of the three parts has an inner design. This does not mean that any person in Bible days followed the current practice of making an outline. It does mean that in olden times, when a leader wished others to follow a prayer, he kept moving forward in the same direction, stage by stage. After a careful study of prayers recorded or reported in Holy Scripture, especially in the Psalms, some of us have never found a single exception to this rule. If the reader wishes a project full of zest and blessing, let him verify the statement by making a study of structure in Bible prayers.

Examples from the Church Hymnal

For examples of structure that calls no attention to itself let us turn to prayer-hymns. Worthy hymns resemble public prayers in this respect: They serve as Christian sacrifices to God. Also, many of our noblest hymns take the form of prayers that voice sanctified feeling. We may pass by hymns that concern only one person and his Lord. These include many of the prayer-hymns that older people love most of all: "Rock of Ages," "Jesus, Lover of My Soul," and "Just as I Am." Each has a simple pattern that not one saint in a hundred ever notices. Among corporate prayer-hymns, any student can figure out the basic design of "O God, Our Help in Ages Past." Like Psalm 90, from which Isaac Watts drew this paraphrase, the hymn has onward motion and cumulative effectiveness, because it follows the lofty purpose of the singer, and does so in an orderly fashion easy to follow.

Another example, widely different, shows a contrasting way of planning a hymn. At Thanksgiving time, on Mother's Day, and often throughout the year, we love to sing "Now Thank We All Our God." Like almost every other noble hymn, this one comes from the Scriptures (Ecclus. 50:20-22). It hails from Germany at a time when that land brought forth noble choral compositions. Written about 1616, the hymn has to do, structurally, with the passing of time. The opening stanza tells of God's goodness, factually, in terms of the past. This part deals with the home, as earth's nearest approach to heaven. The next stanza looks to the future of the persons here present, beseeching the Lord to guide and bless them here on earth, and at last to take them home. Then the third stanza deals with the worshiping people, here and now. Strange to tell, this part of the hymn seems climactic. The song as a whole leads up to a sort of brief hallelujah chorus: "For thus it was, is now, and shall be evermore."

For a still different sort of inner pattern, turn to a prayer-hymn with a Latin original: "Eternal Father, Strong to Save."

155

It has long been used at the Naval Academy in Annapolis, and has become practically the theme song of the United States Navy. The song is also used often on English battleships, and it appears in the hymnbook of the French navy. Of late, through radio and television, the song has become associated with the sinking of the Titanic. At the risk of making moving words seem prosaic, let us set forth the basic pattern. Note the simplicity of the structure, with the use of parallel forms, all of them about the "Three Persons":

I. A Prayer to God the Father
    A. An Ascription of Praise for His Power (3 parts)
    B. A Plea for His Providence Now
II. A Prayer to Christ the Saviour
    A. An Ascription of Praise for His Power (2 parts)
    B. A Plea for His Protection Now
III. A Prayer to the Sacred Spirit
    A. An Ascription of Praise for His Power (3 parts)
    B. A Plea for His Preservation
IV. A Prayer to the Trinity of Love and Power
    A. A Plea for Safety in Peril
    B. For Deliverance from Death
    C. For Hearts Full of Praise to God

Refrain—O hear us when we cry to Thee
        For those in peril on the sea.

A glance over any church hymnal will show that the most beloved songs consist of prayers. Some of them voice the aspirations of an entire congregation. Every one of these prayer-songs has an inconspicuous pattern to which it owes no little of its popular effectiveness. A study of these corporate prayer-songs would show a pleasing variety of patterns. In one hymn the idea of time dominates the design. In another the stress falls on persons, divine and human; among men and women, on one group after another. As a rule, the movement proceeds from the past onward in time, from concerns near at hand to those more remote, and above all, from scenes of earth to the glories of heaven.

After such a survey of prayer-hymns, a minister ought to see the importance of variety in the basic patterns of his public devotions. Ideally, the pastoral prayers of a year ought to differ from one another in structure as much as in that many prayer-hymns. All of these prayers, like all of those supplicating songs, voice much the same human needs, but not merely in one or two mechanical forms.

A Plan for Each Prayer

Before a minister starts to write out a short prayer, he should have in mind a definite purpose. Does he plan to voice the need and the desire for the pardon of sins, for a blessing on the offering, or for the self-dedication of a person who has heard a sermon? With this dominant purpose in mind, the leader should determine whom he plans to address, and in general, how. In every collect, or other brief classic of devotion, one idea dominates the whole, and all the parts move onward in the same direction. Why? Because someone planned the collect that way, perhaps mentally, before he began to write.

Take a secular example of brevity in prose that immediately fixes the mind on one thing, and does not later scatter attention. In Lincoln's Gettysburg Address, he at once sounds the note of dedication. In every part he stresses the same idea, though not continuously with the same words. So in the last paragraph of his Second Inaugural Address, Lincoln shows how to follow a trail in a fashion much different. Here again,

CHAPTER XVI

Preparing to
Pray with Words

THE EFFECTIVENESS OF A PUBLIC PRAYER ALSO DEPENDS ON THE leader's ability to use words for the glory of God and the uplift of His people. However a minister prepares to lead in public worship, the time comes when he utters words which ought to lead the hearts of laymen Godward. Only the best words can begin to be good enough for the public worship of God. Even so, prayers ought not to seem like works of literary art, to be admired because of their form and beauty. No layman can worship God while he is thinking about the leader's mastery of beautiful words.

A public prayer is a corporate act of faith. In it both pastor and people come consciously into the presence of God, and pour out their hearts to Him. Ideally, the minister's use of words should call no more attention to itself than the glass in a window through which a tourist in the Alps looks up to the glory of sunrise on the Matterhorn, sleeping under its mantle of snow. Alas, a prayer may call attention to itself as surely by crudity of form and ugliness of phrasing as by artistic showmanship and beauty of literary style. So it seems once again that every minister should say to his Lord: "Teach me to pray."

Ideals for Public Prayer

Early in the ministry a pastor ought to set up ideals about the style of public prayer. These ideals may come through a study of prayers in the Bible, and of prayer-hymns that the churches of Christendom love to sing. For instance, take "O God, Our Help in Ages Past." These words appeal to learned men so much that the hymn often serves as the processional song in a baccalaureate service at a university chapel, and yet this prayer-song contains no word or phrase difficult for ordinary men and women to comprehend and make their own. Even the boys and girls who attend church soon become accustomed to the only two words not in common use elsewhere: "everlasting" and "eternal." Note the familiar, homely quality of the following terms in the five stanzas that we usually sing:

Help—ages past—hope—years to come—shelter—stormy blast —home—hills—stood—frame—endless years—sight—an evening gone—short as the watch—ends the night—rising sun—ever-rolling stream—bears . . . away—fly—dream—guard—home. [The same home with which the prayer-song begins, but this time in a sense even more dramatic.]

In like manner every public prayer ought to deal with things familiar, but not so as to make them seem commonplace and inconsequential. As a whole, and in every part, a public prayer ought to be interesting. Interesting to whom? To the people whom the minister wishes to lead Godward. A little experience will show that people are more interested in a prayer about persons than in one about abstractions; in one full of facts than in one that abounds in theories; and in one with motion like that of a brook on its way toward the

161

sea, more than in lack of onward movement, as in a pond with no outlet. Worshipers feel far more concern about a child wasting away during a famine in China or India, than about untold millions of emaciated creatures suffering from unknown troubles in inaccessible regions of Asia and Africa. "Words, words, words!" Like Bernard Baruch, "the park-bench statesman," many a skilled leader in prayer might be known as "Dr. Facts." The title comes from Woodrow Wilson, himself a lover of words suitable for public address and corporate prayer.

Most churchgoers today do not think in terms that have been well known to every student of theology. In a sermon, if a minister occasionally employs a technical term, such as omniscience, omnipotence, omnipresence, or transcendence, he can explain what he means by the unfamiliar abstraction. In a prayer, such words ring no bells in the heart of the layman. They awaken no dreams of years bygone, and no hope for days to come. Hence they leave him cold. Among all the prayer-songs in a standard church hymnal, it would be hard to find one that refers to God as solitary, apart from human experience. And yet men have used as a prayer the well-known *Shorter Catechism's* "description of God." Among all of these words about Him, not one suggests anything for a worshiper to see, to feel, to do, or to become:

God is a Spirit, infinite, eternal, and unchangeable, in his being, wisdom, power, holiness, justice, goodness, and truth.

All true, thanks to the erudite Westminster fathers! But almost every one of these words calls for a definition, or perhaps, a description. One of these terms, "being," appears repeatedly in the writings of one of our most profound philosophic theologians, Paul Tillich, and yet only his most devoted followers know what he means by the word "being." To some the term seems to suggest remoteness from human needs and hopes. On the contrary, how does the Fourth Gospel set forth the truth about God? Always with reference to human needs, and often in terms that appeal to the eye of the soul, because they suggest far more than they say. God is Light—Life—Love—Spirit (which may in part mean the Ideal Person)—Father—Like the Lord Jesus. These words also elude definition, but largely because of their mystery they appeal to the heart of every childlike worshiper. They lead us to think of God in terms of our own experience. Every day we have to do with light, with life, with love, with a beloved person, with a worthy father, and with the Lord Jesus.

Thus far we have been thinking about human interest. We have taken for granted that the words of a prayer ought also to be clear to ordinary people, as to their growing boys and girls. Again, every prayer ought to have quiet beauty. Otherwise, how could it make people think rightly toward God, the Creator of all beauty? On a special occasion the prayers may well have the sort of splendor that belongs to Him. Few of us can attain to such heights of expression, but at such times we can borrow majestic prayers from other days. As for quiet beauty, anything of the sort comes best when a minister is thinking about something else. If a leader's heart is moved, and if he lets his heart have its way Godward, simple beauty will come. The beauty of such a prayer has more to do with the modesty of a violet, the glimpse of a fleeting cloud, or the appeal of a baby's smile, than with the stateliness of the gladiolus, the majesty of Niagara Falls, or the silent procession of planets among the stars. As an example of a free prayer, by

163

no means perfect but with quiet beauty, take this from
Hubert Simpson:

We thank Thee for the good things of this life; for food and
raiment and shelter; for work to do and zest in the doing of it;
. . . for the perpetual touch of the divine in life, [and] for the image
of Thyself in the soul of man; for the vigour of youth, the wisdom
of age, and all the lessons of experience; [for] the steps by which
we climb to higher things; for the courage of the brave, the indigna-
tion of the righteous, the kindness of the thoughtful, and all
that makes us men and keeps us Godlike, [through Jesus Christ
our King. Amen.] [1]

Habits of Composition

Early in the ministry every pastor should form lifelong
habits of composing prayers. Ideally, such a discipline ought
to start in the divinity school, where a student begins to set
up ideals about public prayer. But only after a man becomes
responsible for the nurture of a congregation, can he fully
develop the habits now in view. Unlike John Henry Jowett,
the local minister may never become a master of beautiful
words. More like Robert William Dale, the pastor may feel
that with two services every Lord's Day, and many other calls
for public utterance, he can never become known for literary
style. Fortunately, that is not a "man's chief end" in the
ministry. But even the most "selfless" pastor can sense the
difficulty of attaining a style suitable for public prayer. Once
again, listen to Robert William Dale:

Perhaps the most difficult of all styles to acquire is a style perfectly appropriate to public prayer. . . . Not only intelligent and

[1] *Let Us Worship God* (New York: Doubleday, Doran & Co., Inc.,
1928), p. 56.

cultivated men, but very ordinary people, are sensitive to the qualities which render a style suitable to the purposes of devotion. They may find it impossible to explain why it is that when they are listening to one man's prayers their hearts are filled with awe and reverence and devout trust, and that when they are listening to the prayers of another man, who is not less devout, they find it almost impossible to pray at all; but the difference in the mere style of the prayers may often suggest a partial explanation of the difficulty.[2]

The difficulty may be due to the difference between the language of prayer and that of preaching. This distinction a young minister can learn by working for a while with an older pastor who knows how to pray and to preach. To us at Princeton Seminary a young man came from Canada to do graduate work. Soon he made us feel that he knew how to lead in prayer without seeming to preach. In answer to a question in private he explained that for a term of years he had served as assistant to a pastor in Toronto, who had required him to prepare for this part of his ministry on the Lord's Day, and had gradually led him to see the difference between the style of a prayer and that of a sermon. Many another seminary graduate can do much the same thing during his first pastorate. He can set up at home a "school for the soul," with the Holy Spirit as Teacher and Guide.

The self-discipline ought to include mastery of the paragraph. In all present-day prose worthy of the name, the paragraph serves as the unit of thought or feeling. In a public prayer, as a rule, a man should confine himself to a single paragraph. In it he should address the Deity only once. Such a paragraph may never qualify as a literary gem, but it can embody a single vital element of prayer, such as Adoration or

[2] Op. cit., pp. 171-72.

Confession. The dominant note ought to sound forth at the beginning, keep on ringing out in each successive sentence, and reach a climax at the end. Such a paragraph may run to a hundred words, or a few more. If it goes much further, the paragraph may call attention to itself through overweight, and thus defeat its purpose of leading every heart Godward.

In the study a man schools himself to work with the paragraph as a unit in the corporate expression of feeling, much as he plans the inner development of a sermon, with the paragraph as the unit of thought. When he goes into the House of Prayer to lead others heavenward, he should not think about paragraphs; but all unknown to himself at the time, he will set forth each element of ongoing emotion in such a way that everyone present will enter easily into the spirit of prayer, and without effort follow on to the end, which ought to come before attention begins to lag. On the other hand, if the paragraph ended too soon, it would not adequately express any holy emotion.

It is much more difficult to write about the sentences in a prayer. One thing we shall take for granted: Sentences in a prayer should differ from those in a sermon. In a prayer they may run longer, but they should never seem wild and loose. The element of parallelism may enter still more largely into the sentences of a prayer. In the example above from Hubert Simpson, the paragraph consists of a single sentence, with a succession of parallel clauses easy for a layman to follow. Brevity comes through the omission of the repetitions common in many prayers. If only for practice, try breaking up such a compact paragraph into six or eight sentences, each with the customary complement of subject and predicate. Then note the wisdom of avoiding "meaningless repetitions."

The chief difference between sentences in prayer and those

in preaching has to do with rhythm. As we have already seen, emotion in prayer normally expresses itself in words that flow. In such onward motion they assume the form of sentences. Within each paragraph the sentences keep flowing in the same direction, with clauses more or less alike, resembling waves that keep tumbling up on the beach, until at last they reach their crest, when the movement subsides, but does not cease. Perhaps unfortunately, a love of rhythmical prose must be caught; it cannot be taught.

A sense of prose rhythm in public prayer comes best to a minister who has learned to enjoy Hebrew poetry in the original, with its parallelism and its musical flow. For a lover of liturgy the study of rhythm should also include the sonorous tones of Latin devotions. The leader in free prayer should thank God even more if in youth he has learned to enjoy the Anglo-Saxon rhythm of *Beowulf* and the Middle English rhythm of Chaucer's *Canterbury Tales*. Even without such early schooling a pastor can learn much about rhythm by reading aloud the poetry of the Bible, and by saturating his soul in other classic poetry. He should live with the music of Bach, Beethoven, and Brahms, and in numerous other ways become a lover of beauty. "Let the beauty of the Lord our God be upon us." (Ps. 90:17a.)

The Mastery of Words

As distinct from preaching, the style of public prayer differs most of all in the choice and the use of words. Here again, anyone can sense the difference; no one can explain it. "The literature of feeling" consists of words that differ from those in "the literature of thought." Here we can think only about free prayer, which makes no claim to be classic literature. Someone suggests that prayers in church ought to in-

167

clude only such words as appear in the King James Version. That would be going too far, but in the right direction. The language of a prayer ought to differ from that of a shop, or a ball park. In the old King James, or in any other noteworthy version, a minister does well to study the words of Bible prayers. For example, take a corporate prayer, Ps. 90; or a personal prayer, Ps. 51. In the central part of the latter psalm (vss. 7-9) note the following words full of feeling:

Purge — clean — wash — whiter — snow — hear — gladness — bones — broken — rejoice — hide — face — blot out.

The stress here falls on the nouns and the verbs. There is a paucity of descriptive adjectives and adverbs. The nouns have strength. The verbs are full of motion. Whether or not they embody figures of speech, these words suggest much to see, to hear, to feel, to become. Such terms have become known as "live words," "words with hands and feet." They tell of something strong, and they show the meaning while they move. They march, and that to music often martial. They also suggest far more than they say. Hence this penitential psalm leads up to a petition that a minister on his knees in the study can make his own: "O Lord, open thou my lips; and my mouth shall shew forth thy praise" (Ps. 51:15).

One may also study the prayer-hymns of the Church. For instance, take a song of supplication, "Spirit of God, Descend Upon My Heart," by George Croly. This hymn contains only two words not in common use today: "ecstasies" and "visitant," and yet the song does not impress anyone as commonplace. It has more than a few "live words," or "fact words": descend — wean — pulses — move — stoop — dream — rending—veil—clay—angel—opening—skies—dimness. And so on to the word picture at the end: "My heart an altar, and Thy love the flame."

If a man carried these ideas about beauty too far, his prayers might become flowery. Most of us need not dread any tendency toward "fine writing." We are far too prosaic. We need to watch our words. As a rule, in making ready for a public prayer, one should give the preference to a short word rather than a long one; to a word that tells about a person or a concrete fact, not about some abstract idea, such as sovereignty or integration; to a word that appeals to the "eye of the soul," not mainly to thinking powers; to the Anglo-Saxon rather than the Latin or the Greek, thus excluding technical terms that end in ation, ism, and ology. Gradually one can make up a private *Index Expurgatorius* of terms to be banned from public prayer. One man's list begins with "particularly," a word particularly hard to pronounce. With it go out such words as "individual," "reaction," "characteristic," and so on, almost *ad nauseam*.

"Take with you words, and turn to the Lord." (Hos. 14:2.) In simple terms full of beauty, near the end of a heart-warming book, the prophet is here calling for a revival. He is beseeching the people to pray, and in prayer to confess their sins. Here and elsewhere the prophet of love employs terms suitable for public worship. When a minister leads in public prayer, he ought never to think about his use of words. In private conversation he can school himself to speak nothing but the King's English. In the study, often on his knees, he can learn how to pray with words for the glory of the God to whom he speaks, and for the blessing of the friends whose desires he voices. Just before he enters the House of Prayer, he may kneel down and utter a petition for himself as the leader of the waiting congregation:

O Lord our God, forasmuch as without Thee I am not able to please Thee, meet me with Thy Holy Spirit as I enter the holy place, that I may pray to Thee in sincerity and worship Thee in truth, and that, my mind and heart being ruled by Thee, I may in everything fulfill Thy will and glorify Thy name, through Jesus Christ, my Lord.[3]

[3] From *The Book of Common Order* by permission of the Church of Scotland Committee on Public Worship and Aids to Devotion.

CHAPTER XVII

Speaking to God in His House

AT LAST WE COME TO THE HOUR OF PUBLIC WORSHIP. IT IN-cludes music, readings, and a sermon, but here we can think only about the prayers. Under God, their effectiveness and helpfulness depend much on the way the leader approaches this part of his privileges as the local representative of the Most High. He should look on the hour of morning worship as the most important part of the week, and on his opportunity to lead in prayer as a privilege second to none on earth, especially when he leads in celebration of the sacraments, or in observance of the ordinances. How then should he utter prayers in this hour of uplift and triumph?

An Approach to God

On the Lord's Day the minister's prayer for others may begin when he meets with the choir. At other times he should get to know the singers by name, and thank them for their services of love. Just before the climactic hour of the week, he should enter the choir room inconspicuously, not as a jolly good fellow, but as a man intent on important business for the King. After a few words of prayer, he should leave the singers in the mood of holy expectation. According to a wise man of old, "There is . . . a time to every purpose under the heaven: . . . a time to weep, and a time to laugh; . . . a time to keep silence, and a time to speak" (Eccl. 3:1, 4, 7). These few moments with the Lord's appointed singers call for only a few words of prayer, with nothing frivolous before or after. One time there may be a collect, such as the well-known one beginning: "Almighty God, unto whom all hearts are open." Usually there should be a prayer composed by the minister; for example:

O Lord, we bless Thee for a faith that teaches us to sing, to pray, and to hope. We thank Thee for these friends whom Thou hast called to the holy ministry of song. We beseech Thee to bless this hour of public worship, and every heart open before Thee in Thy House, through Jesus Christ, in whose name we sing and pray and hope. Amen.

Following the choir the pastor may go into the House of Prayer. Inconspicuously he should take the place appointed for the leader of worship. Reverently he should bow down or kneel in prayer, according to the local custom. Never should he look out over the waiting congregation to count the number present, or nod to certain friends. Neither should he worry about the weather, the empty pews, gradually to be filled by latecomers, or anything else. All of these matters deserve his attention, but not now. In the holy of holies he should have no eye and no thought for anyone but the King.

During the Prelude the time calls for contemplation of God's mercy in setting apart this hour in the holy of holies. The Call to Prayer ought to sound forth, not with a loud voice, but with glad assurance that God stands ready to bless all those who "come boldly to the throne of grace, that [they] may obtain mercy, and find grace to help in time of need"

(Heb. 4:16). The few words of Adoration call for a spirit of awe and wonder, which ought to prove contagious. The Confession of Sins requires a different tone, with a spirit of solemnity because of sorrow, leading up to the expression of relief and joy because the sins truly confessed have found pardon and cleansing.

From this time forward, through changing scenes in the drama of redemption, now being re-enacted, the "tone color" of the speaking should vary, one can scarcely tell how. Everywhere, except in the Confession and in portions of the General Prayer, the prevailing mood should be "apostolic optimism." In Old Testament times public worship began with sacrificial ways of getting right with God. Then it called on His people to enjoy their religion. How much more should we Christians enjoy, and not merely endure, the hour in which we celebrate redemption wrought by the Death and the Resurrection of our Lord, the sense of His living presence through the Holy Spirit, and the assurance of His Final Return, to complete the work actively begun at the Incarnation!

Take an example of speaking in different ways during the same service. Think of a marriage in a church where God is uniting in holy wedlock a young man and a young woman whom He has chosen for each other. When speaking to the groom, in the name of his God, the pastor may use tones suggestive of stability and strength. When the minister turns to the bride, and speaks the very same words, he may utter them with overtones of "sweetness and light." Much more, in speaking to God on behalf of His redeemed children assembled on the Lord's Day to receive His blessing, the minister ought to let the spirit of what he is saying guide in the way he utters varying shades of emotion. If his heart is on fire and under loving control, he can let his feelings have their way. Rarely

173

will they fail to voice the inner spirit of what he is putting into words. A sense of God's presence and desire to bless ought to fill the leader's heart with the Gospel of hope. No matter how stormy the day, or how gloomy the times, down in the valleys where people have to live and toil, and where some of them have to suffer and die, in church the pastor should lead in prayer as a radiant believer in the goodness of God, and as one who already has entered into the mysteries of the unseen world. Such a radiant spirit goes far to make an hour in church a mountaintop experience, when worshiping people behold their King, and are changed into His likeness.

Awareness of the Worshipers

The leader in prayer ought ever to speak with regard for the worshiping people. Especially for the sake of elderly folk dull of hearing, he should make every word of a prayer easily audible. If not, all unintentionally he may cause attendance at church to become for them a burden, not a delight. If the lay officers install an amplifying machine, he should learn how to speak through it so as not to jar the nerves of those whose hearing is acute. His voice should be natural and pleasing, not nasal and rasping. He should not stress a word or a phrase by raising the pitch and increasing the volume. As he grows more intense in pleas for the overthrow of evil in Russia and elsewhere, why should he become noisy, even bombastic?

"The Lord God hath given me the tongue of the learned, that I should know how to speak." (Isa. 50:4.) In the original these words point to a prophetic ministry by the Servant of the Lord, but the same principle applies to every leader in prayer. If he does not know how to say what the Lord has put into his heart, the minister is not yet properly educated

174

for his lifework. And yet among all the books about public worship, scarcely one devotes attention to the way a minister should speak to God in prayer. The reason for such silence may be that some books of the sort are made up from other books that do not raise questions difficult to answer.

Suggestions looking toward the answer come from a study of I Kings 18. There the prophet Elijah enters into a contest with prophets of Baal. After they have failed to bring down fire to consume their pagan sacrifice, he taunts them about their ways of addressing Baal: "Cry aloud: for he is a god; either he is talking, or he is pursuing, or he is in a journey, or peradventure he sleepeth, and must be awaked" (vs. 27). So they cry aloud, and cut themselves, but despite all their acts of desperation, they cannot bring down fire from their "no-god." On the other hand, with mighty feelings under firm control, Elijah gathers the people about him, speaks to them with calm assurance, and when all things are ready, prays to God for fire, which comes down to consume the waiting sacrifice. What a warning against bombast!

In other words, the way a man prays in public shows people the sort of Person he worships, and the way he regards that Person. The leader cannot change his God-given temperament, or the basic quality of his voice. But he can school himself to make the most of his personality, and to use his voice as an effective way of representing people before God. Jowett had a tenor voice that he could use in prayer with as much beauty and effectiveness as Spurgeon or Beecher attained with a lower voice that must have had almost as many tones as a pipe organ. Whatever the original voice equipment, the ways of effective leaders in prayer suggest a few observations.

Ability to make oneself heard in prayer depends far more on

benediction tend to dispel these hallowed impressions, with both pastor and people. In deference to custom he goes to the main entrance and shakes hands with persons on their way homeward. While innocent, much of the conversation with these passers-by does not seem to be uplifting, or even religious. In our zeal to promote friendliness, and to make visitors feel at home, we Protestants often take away the glow from the recollections of uplifting worship, especially the prayers. After a moving scene on the Mount of Transfiguration (Matt. 17:1-8), if the disciples had begun to talk about the weather, no one of them would have remembered that momentous experience through all his later years (cf. II Pet. 1:17).

In more than one church the minister follows another course. After the benediction, and brief music from the organ, he stands before the pulpit, or the altar. There he quietly welcomes anyone who comes forward to share a special burden, or to bring happy news about a loved one dear to the heart of the pastor. Another person wishes to arrange for a conference about his doubts, or something else in the General Prayer. Still others, not many on any one day, merely wish to greet the minister and wish him Godspeed. Whatever the nature of these few words in passing, the hush of the church, and the touch of his loving hand, tend to keep alive, and even to heighten, the hallowed impressions of the hour with God in the House of Prayer.

A final word may have to do with the blessing of God on all that the minister says and does for Him in public prayer. Like the prophet Elijah on Mount Carmel (I Kings 18:17-39), the pastor and the other leaders in public worship strive to do all things well. They build the altar, or else keep it in worthy shape. On it they lay the best wood they can find, and the most acceptable sacrifice. They need never think about cold water, for someone not far away will be sure to find fault. In short, as a leader of churchmen, the pastor may do all that his redeemed powers enable him to do, and do it in ways pleasing to the Holy One. Most of all, like the prophet on Carmel, the pastor himself should rely on prayer.

God alone can send the fire that should attend an hour of worship. Through the Holy Spirit, He alone can change a passing glow of emotion into a flame of transforming fire. Today, as on Mount Carmel, transforming grace comes in response to a minister's public prayers. "The God that answereth by fire, let him be God!"

CHAPTER XVIII

Getting the
People to Pray

UNDER GOD, THE FINAL TEST OF A MINISTER'S PUBLIC PRAYERS
relates to the people who attend church. While he is uttering
prayers in their name, and on their behalf, are they praying?
Or are they merely listening to him, as they would hang onto
the words of a Shakespearean actor posing as Hamlet? In a
worse case, do they listen at all? To take an actual experience,
do they resemble college girls in a report about a passing procession of peripatetic pulpiteers who held forth in Sunday
chapel week after week? "If we like the first sentence or two
of a man's prayers, we keep on listening. Usually we don't
care to hear anything more, so we start thinking about something nice." More than one of them went out wool-gather-
ing, and assembled enough golden fleece to weave a gorgeous
robe for some hypothetical Prince Charming. Elsewhere more
prosaic businessmen, long after college years, may listen to the
sermon, but take time out during the prayers. They find
it more interesting to think about business deals, or else about
golf.

Lay Attitudes During Public Prayer

Why do many churchgoers not pay attention during the
prayers? Especially during the most important one of all,

why do they think about something else? With few exceptions adults who attend church wish to become better men and women. Almost every one of them could cry out with Tennyson:

> And ah for a man to arise in me,
> That the man I am may cease to be!

According to a well-known saying by William James, many a man comes to the House of Prayer feeling "consciously wrong, inferior, unhappy." He longs to go out from church feeling "consciously right, superior, happy." And yet we sometimes refer to such an earnest seeker after God as a "hardheaded businessman."

Down in his heart the man now before us wishes that he could pray, both in public and at home. When the church has a minister whom the layman respects and likes, he may begin to hope that at last he will learn to pray. Someday in church he discovers that he has begun to follow the General Prayer. The pastor is guiding worshipers over hills and down through valleys of human experience, and out on uplands where everyone feels that God is near, and that He cares. The leader is not making an "eloquent and scholarly prayer"; he is using words that even a novice in devotion can follow with case. Soon the layman will become a learner in the school of Christ. From this point onward, his growth in this Christian grace will largely depend on the leadership of a pastor who knows how to pray in public. Such a minister rightly looks on himself as a home missionary of prayer.

How can a pastor tell whether or not the majority of those who attend church enter into the prayers, or merely endure his performance? Only God can read these human hearts. However, He may guide the leader in forming certain im-

181

pressions. If little by little people begin coming to church ahead of time, he may infer that they wish to enter actively into the opening prayer. If after church more than one bashful saint thanks him for an item in the General Prayer, he should not feel flattered, but grateful. As with passing remarks about sermons, he learns to take some compliments with several grains of salt, not to say suspicion, according to the source. On the contrary, some people mean what they say. If they always refer to him as "the preacher," and never as a man of prayer, he may ask himself whether he resembles the Master, who taught His disciples to pray.

A minister becomes known as a pastor, a preacher, or a man of prayer. Ideally, he should combine the three, and likewise serve as a church leader who gets the people to do the Lord's work. Into Kentucky went such a young man of average ability, an "all-round" minister who never could win distinction. Greeting him at first as a stranger from afar, before three months the young people came to him in a group and said to him, quietly: "Pastor, teach us to pray." Like the disciples of old, those young folk did not ask him to teach them *how*. They seemed to feel that if they learned to pray, and kept on praying, they would "learn how to do by doing."

When a minister gets the people to pray aright, in public and in private, through them he can accomplish anything good that the Lord wishes pastor and people to do for Him. On the contrary, ministers everywhere agree that in as far as they can judge things spiritual, the members of the home church, individually and collectively, seem to be weaker in their prayer life than in any other respect. Many an indefatigable pastor would confess that amid all his multitudinous endeavors he has done little or nothing to remedy this weakness in the home church. If he were a family physician, and if he felt that the well-being of his patients depended on their having abundance of fresh air and sunshine, he would devote time and attention to the promotion of living in God's out-of-doors. In things of the Spirit, this means Bible reading and prayer.

For weakness in the prayer life of the local church we who teach and write books about practical theology must bear some of the blame. Often we stress human methods, rather than divine power. In a book about *Pastoral Leadership* I devoted a chapter to "The Goals of a Pastorate." Every one of those eight goals still stands firm, but there should have been one more. According to an appreciative review, by an able teacher of young ministers, the chapter should also have dealt with getting church people to pray. As for ways of attaining such a goal, man-made books tell but little. Fortunately, the most practical New Testament author shows a part of the secret: "If any of you lacks wisdom, let him ask God, who gives to all men generously and without reproaching, and it will be given him. But let him ask in faith, with no doubting." (Jas. 1:5-6a R.S.V.)

Prayer in the Family Circle

Under the leadership of the pastor every home should become a "house of prayer." Under Richard Baxter something of the sort took place at Kidderminster, a village in central England. According to reliable sources, in 1641 when he went there, practically no household had a family altar. Nineteen years later, when he left that humble village and went to London, almost every family in Kidderminster assembled daily for prayers. In no small measure because of those family devotions, the community became transformed. Much the same held true at rural Kilmany in Scotland. After seven years of fruitless ministry, Thomas Chalmers, the pastor, began to put God first, and to live with his Bible prayerfully. Then the people, too, began to pray, both at church and in their homes. They learned increasingly to exalt Christ, and to do His will. Hence Kilmany became transformed. So it seems that a praying minister can get churchgoers to pray, especially at the family altar.

Such pastoral guidance may come in premarital counseling. When a young man and his beloved call on a minister to arrange for their marriage, he can encourage them to pray for each other. He can also emphasize the importance of their establishing the new home on a Christian foundation of Bible reading and prayer. According to Augustine of Hippo, when our Lord spoke about two persons praying together (Matt. 18:19), He referred to a young husband and his bride. They should pray together, aloud, on the evening of their marriage day. Both of them may be thinking about something else, but they can pray together about that. As our Lord teaches, "God made them male and female. For this cause shall a man leave his father and mother, and cleave to his wife; And they twain shall be one flesh." (Mark 10:6b-8a.)

A year or so later this home welcomes a baby. According to Augustine, when our Lord spoke about three as praying together, He referred to a young father and mother praying over their first newborn babe. The blessing of God abides on a child who from birth, and even before, has been nurtured in prayer, which finds expression by day at the family altar and by night at the baby's crib. A psychologist may write about such things in terms of the unconscious; the Scriptures ascribe them to God's blessing on prayer, and on other ways of child nurture in the Lord (Deut. 6:4-9). Biography shows that from such homes come nearly all our noblest pastors and missionaries, with hosts of consecrated laymen.

Back of such a home lies the influence of a pastor. By example and by precept he trains people to pray. He may tell a prospective bride and groom about two ways of conducting family worship. After the morning meal, when time may run short, they can use a page in the *Upper Room*, or some other booklet intended to guide in family devotions. Or they can use the prayer book of some church, which may not be their own. After the evening meal they can follow a better plan, because it uses the Bible as it was written, one book at a time, and in passage after passage. The father, or the mother, reads a paragraph or two from Luke, or some other portion of Holy Writ. Then one of them, preferably the father, leads in prayer.

When the little ones get old enough to talk, they should take part in family devotions. If at night father and mother repeat from memory a psalm, a parable, or a hymn, a wee boy or girl gradually learns it by heart. So a child can join in family prayers, especially by asking the blessing at times before they eat together. Meanwhile young married folk need to learn from their pastor that family devotions, like secret prayers, mean talking things over with the heavenly Father, in words and sentences simple enough for a six-year-old boy to follow. Such prayers call for no erudition and no eloquence. In the words of St. Teresa, "The life of prayer is just love to God, and the custom of being ever with Him."

In a large Lutheran congregation of Chicago a certain pastor set up as an objective having a family altar in every home. By catechetical teaching, by pastoral calling, by sermons, and by other means, as opportunity offered, he promoted the custom of daily household devotions. Whenever he deemed such a course necessary, he went to a home about nine o'clock at night and showed the people there how to conduct devotions simply and helpfully. Most of all he relied on the Lord's blessing, and on the pastoral art of expecting much from people, in God's name. In time he estimated that 90 per cent of the homes in the parish held family devotions every day, many of them twice a day. In a smaller church, such a plan would work even better, as it once did at Kidderminster and at Kilmany.

Prayer in the Secret Place

"Behold, he prayeth!" (Acts 9:11c.) So said the Holy Spirit long ago about "public enemy number one" of the newborn Christian Church. That man of nearly middle age had doubtless been "saying prayers" all his life. Then one day on the Damascus Road, while he was "hell-bent" on "liquidating" believers in Christ—both men and women—Saul of Tarsus met the living Christ, face to face. Immediately the persecutor surrendered to the risen Lord. Soon after his blinding shock the new recruit began to pray, alone with his God. Amid all "the varieties of religious experience," the pastor may never encounter a case like that of Saul. Even so, whenever a worldly or a wicked man gives himself into the keeping of the hands that once were pierced, he needs the tender care of a man like Ananias, who has known the Lord for years, and has learned to pray.

In a small congregation the minister can know the people well. If he remains at home and takes loving care of the flock, he can help any person who needs encouragement and guidance about secret prayer. Little by little, through joining in prayers at church, the seeker after a "closer walk with God" finds that the minister can pray, and that he wants to help every person who needs a prayer guide. Often the change to a life of devotion comes to a layman during convalescence from a serious illness, such as a coronary thrombosis. Then, if ever, the physician of souls can get behind the barrier of reserve, or timidity, that has kept the layman from counseling with his spiritual mentor.

Better still, the pastor can deal with boys and girls in the beauty of life's morning. Both directly, in a pastor's class, and indirectly, through appointed workers with these little ones, he can lead them into habits of secret prayer. As a sort of working motto he can hold up these words from a psalm about old age: "O satisfy us early with thy mercy, that we may rejoice and be glad all our days" (Ps. 90:14).

Promoting Prayer in a Large Church

In a large congregation the senior pastor may have to delegate many of these privileges. If only for the good of his soul, and the increase of his usefulness, he dare not relinquish all these pastoral ministries. In the Middle West at a state university with fifteen thousand students the president told his young pastor: "I cannot know them all, intimately, but I aim to know well at least a thousand." This thousand consisted largely of those who came to him for personal counsel. He is said to have been the last of the oldtime university presidents who showed concern about many individual students. Because of those personal contacts, and the loving heart that they revealed, he became a spiritual power on the campus, throughout the state, and far beyond.

In a large congregation a minister can follow much the same course, with special emphasis on getting people, one by one, to pray. At the First Baptist Church of Richmond, Virginia, Theodore F. Adams has become known afar as an "all-round minister," or "pastoral director." Of course he delegates to other members of the staff, and to lay leaders, most of the church business. He himself serves as the main promoter of prayer, especially in the secret place. The people must feel that he knows how to pray in private as well as in public. Year after year, in June, when they have an opportunity to choose among the sermons of the year which two they wish him to repeat on a given Lord's Day, they always select one message about prayer, and often two. The second one comes at the regular evening service, which seems not to be a problem in a church where the people love to pray.

What Karl Barth has said about the Reformers holds true of such a pastor and his people. They not only believe in prayer; they pray. Under the leadership of a minister who puts the promotion of Bible reading and prayer ahead of everything else, except evangelism, an atmosphere of devotion tends to prevail throughout the congregation as a whole, and in every household. In meetings of the Official Board, as among wee tots in the Beginners' Department of the Bible School, everything is begun, continued, and completed in prayer. All the worship, the teaching, and the work proceed on a basis distinctly Christian. Among other evidences of God's favor, money for Kingdom enterprises keeps pouring into the treasury. Why not? The people love the Lord, they enjoy their religion, and they find joy in giving through the church dear to their hearts. In brief, they have a minister who prays, and who gets the people to pray.

A congregation that consists of praying people is sure to abound in every good work. In prayer they "seek first the kingdom of God, and his righteousness" (Matt. 6:33). Then they trust Him to supply "all these things" to which our Lord refers as by-products of living first for God. In this part of the Sermon on the Mount our Lord refers to "things that money can buy." He does not mean that they come automatically, but that in prayer the Kingdom seekers ascertain the will of God, and then do it gladly. In the well-known words of William Carey, "Expect great things from God; attempt great things for God."

As a leader Dwight L. Moody showed the practical workings of such a Christian philosophy. In prayer he learned to "expect great things from God." As a Christian leader, and a promoter of good works, he showed what it meant to "attempt great things for God," and in prayer to rely on Him to provide all the needed resources. God never failed to respond through His people who prayed. The stress did not fall on men, machinery, and money, but on God and His grace, with giving for the Kingdom, in the spirit of prayer and joyous service. Moody could have learned all this from Spurgeon.

Early in their married life Spurgeon and his bride learned through prayer to rely on God for the supply of all their domestic needs. Throughout his later years Spurgeon followed this principle of trusting God to provide for manifold enterprises involving the expenditure of money in vast amounts. At the Tabernacle he gathered about him a host of people who not only believed in prayer, but who prayed. To a younger minister from the United States the London pastor revealed the secret of his effectiveness as the leader of a church with what must have seemed like an impossible program. This younger man, J. Wilbur Chapman, discovered that the power lay chiefly in the prayer life of the congregation. Whenever Chapman tried to congratulate Spurgeon on any stupendous achievement, the latter would reply, in substance: "Tut, tut! Don't praise me! Every morning and evening, and often at other times, all these people, and hosts of others elsewhere, keep praying for me and for this work at the Tabernacle. In keeping with His promise, God opens the windows of heaven and pours out blessings so many and vast that there is not room to receive them all. So give the glory to Him."

The same principle applies to the work of a minister who may never become famous, and to a church that may never grow large. Most ministers and congregations have the heavenly "treasure in earthen vessels," neither large nor costly (cf. I Cor. 1:26-31). So if any man wishes to lead a church of average size in doing a large work for the Kingdom, the surest way to carry out such a program is to promote congregational Bible reading and prayer, in the power of the Cross. By these spiritual means a pastor can lead Christlike people to accept any known duty, and to perform it gloriously, as a high spiritual privilege.

The practical philosophy that undergirds this chapter, and this entire book, stands out in the Epistle to the Ephesians, "The Living Christ in His Church." This "prison epistle" seems to have been a "circular letter," addressed to a number of "young churches" and their ministers. The first three chapters set forth the heart of the Gospel; the last three show the application to the practical affairs of life, especially in a Christian home. In the doctrinal half the climactic paragraph embodies a prayer by the Apostle for one of these new congregations, as a vital part of "the holy Church throughout all the world." These words any pastor can make his own, while interceding for the home congregation:

For this cause [in view of all that God in Christ has done and is doing through the Gospel] I bow my knees unto the Father of our Lord Jesus Christ, Of whom the whole family in heaven and earth is named, That he would grant you, according to the riches of his glory, to be strengthened with might by his Spirit in the inner man; That Christ may dwell in your hearts by faith; that ye, being rooted and grounded in love, May be able to comprehend with all saints what is the breadth, and length, and depth, and height; and to know the love of God, which passeth knowledge, that ye might be filled with all the fulness of God.

Now unto him that is able to do exceeding abundantly above all that we ask or think, according to the power that worketh in us, Unto him be glory in the church throughout all ages, world without end. Amen. (Eph. 3:14-21.)

Check List of
Faults in Public Prayer

Lack of Reality

—— Not praying: Not speaking to God on behalf of people.

—— Parroting: Mechanically repeating prayers by other men.

—— Quoting: Reciting at random from the Bible and the hymnal.

—— Private Devotions: Conducting one's personal devotions aloud.

Mistakes in Purpose

—— Preaching: Striving to influence people; not speaking to God.

—— Teaching: Trying to explain a passage, a truth, or a duty.

—— Exhorting: Seeking to promote personal morale, or church work.

—— Flattering: Paying homage to a person, living or departed.

—— Rebuking: Attacking certain persons or movements.

Errors in Attitude

—— Dramatic: Making an exhibition of God-given abilities.

193

_____ Artistic: Calling attention to one's mastery of English.

_____ Perfunctory: Going through religious acts at appointed times.

_____ Professional: Assuming an air of authority; posing as an expert.

_____ Apologetic: Pleading with people to do what God enjoins.

_____ Flippant: Showing no signs of reverence, dignity, or decorum.

_____ Slovenly: Ignoring conventions of church, community, and culture.

Weakness of Content

_____ Shallowness: Relying on "words without thoughts."

_____ Iteration: Thoughtlessly repeating names of the Deity.

_____ Generalities: Not speaking personally and factually.

_____ Overlapping: Saying the same things from prayer to prayer.

_____ Overlooking: Failing to voice basic needs of those present.

_____ Favoritism: Ignoring the needs of certain groups.

_____ Parochialism: Neglecting to pray for others elsewhere.

Defects in Structure

_____ Foresight: Having no basic plan for the entire service.

_____ System: Making no plan for each successive prayer.

_____ Inner Order: Failing to arrange the parts of a prayer.

_____ Continuity: Not tying in with what precedes or follows.

_____ Progress: Arranging no onward motion from prayer to prayer.

_____ Climax: Leaving no sense of arrival and completeness.

Lapses in Form

—— Feeling: Failing to show feeling, or letting it go wild.

—— "Tone Color": Not conveying the spirit of each prayer.

—— Sentences: Letting sentences run loose, long, and wild.

—— Phrases: Using the clichés of men in times bygone.

—— Words: Employing terms abstract and impersonal, not vital.

—— Grammar: Departing from present English idiom: "We pray Thy blessing upon"; "Forgive us of our sins"; "We ask that we might."

Faults in Speaking

—— Appearance: Showing no signs of peace, self-control, joy.

—— Affectation: Adopting a "holy tone"; using affected speech.

—— Familiarity: Addressing the Lord caressingly: "Jé-sús."

—— Arrogance: "Backing Him into a corner; laying down the law."

—— Showmanship: Calling attention chiefly to oneself.

—— Intonation: Falling into a monotone; using singsong.

—— Tempo: Resorting to rapid utterance, often indistinct.

—— Volume: Trying to show feeling by loudness, or shouting.

—— Pitch: Letting the voice keep rising to a nasal shriek.

—— Fading Out: Not sustaining the voice at the end of a sentence.

—— Pronunciation: Departing from usage: "Gawd," "glawry," "strenth."

—— Time: Exceeding the limits of prudence and good taste.

Failure with the People

—— Primacy: Not putting prayer at the heart of church life.

—— Attendance: Not securing regular, prompt attendance at church.

—— Reverence: Not promoting the spirit of worship in God's House.

—— Participation: Not leading people to pray with the pastor.

—— Ideals: Not fostering a desire to pray in secret.

—— Family Prayers: Not helping people set up a family altar.

—— Prayer Life: Not developing a congregation that prays.

—— Basic Causes: Lack of ministerial piety, culture, or training.

———————

"My people are destroyed for lack of knowledge." (Hos. 4: 6a A.R.V.)
"It shall be, like people, like priest." (Vs. 9a.)

Selected List
of Related Readings

PUBLIC WORSHIP

Abba, Raymond. *Principles of Christian Worship*. New York: Oxford University Press, 1957.

Blackwood, Andrew W. *The Fine Art of Public Worship*. Nashville: Abingdon Press, 1939.

Calvin, John. *Institutes of the Christian Religion*. Tr. John Allen. Grand Rapids: William B. Eerdmans Publishing Co., 1949.

Coffin, Henry Sloane. *The Public Worship of God*. Philadelphia: The Westminster Press, 1946.

Cullmann, Oscar. *Early Christian Worship*. Tr. A. Stewart Todd and James B. Torrance. London: S.C.M. Press, 1953.

Davies, Horton. *Christian Worship—Its History and Meaning*. Nashville: Abingdon Press, 1957.

Duchesne, Louis Marie Olivier. *Christian Worship*. New York: The Macmillan Co., 1903.

Hislop, D. H. *Our Heritage in Public Worship*. New York: Charles Scribner's Sons, 1935.

Horn, Edward Traill. *The Christian Year*. Philadelphia: Muhlenberg Press, 1957.

Jones, Ilion T. *A Historical Approach to Evangelical Worship*. Nashville: Abingdon Press, 1954.

Maxwell, William D. *An Outline of Christian Worship*. New

York: Oxford University Press, 1939. Historical development.

Micklem, Nathaniel (ed.). *Christian Worship*. New York: Oxford University Press, 1936.

Otto, Rudolf. *The Idea of the Holy*. Tr. J. W. Harvey. 2nd ed. New York: Oxford University Press, 1950.

Underhill, Evelyn. *Worship*. New York: Harper & Bros., 1957. A "Torchbook." Paper.

Wallis, Charles L. (comp.). *Worship Resources for the Christian Year*. New York: Harper & Bros., 1954.

Will, Robert. *Le Culte*. 3 vols. Strasbourg: Librarie Istra, 1925-35.

PUBLIC PRAYER

Bowie, Walter Russell. *Lift Up Your Hearts*. Enlarged ed. Nashville: Abingdon Press, 1956.

Edwards, Charles E. (comp.). *Devotions and Prayers of John Calvin*. Grand Rapids: Baker Book House, 1954.

Gray, Walter G. *Prayers for the Pulpit*. Westwood, N.J.: Fleming H. Revell Co., 1957.

Halsey, Jesse (ed.). *Open Prayer*. Nashville: Abingdon Press, 1951.

Micklem, Nathaniel (ed.). *Prayers and Praises*. London: Independent Press, Ltd., 1955.

Noyes, Morgan P. (ed.). *Prayers for Services*. New York: Charles Scribner's Sons, 1934.

Prayers for the Christian Year. 2nd ed. New York: Oxford University Press, 1952. Prepared for the Church of Scotland by the Committee on Public Worship and Aids to Devotion of the Church of Scotland.

Schmiechen, Samuel J. *Pastoral Prayers for the Church Year*. Nashville: Abingdon Press, 1957.

Steere, Douglas Van. *Prayer and Worship*. New York: Association Press, 1938. Quaker ideals.

Suter, John W. (ed.). *A Book of English Collects*. New York: Harper & Bros., 1941.

Tittle, Ernest F. *A Book of Pastoral Prayers*. Nashville: Abingdon Press, 1951.

Todd, James M. *Prayers and Services for Christian Festivals*. New York: Oxford University Press, 1951.

Watts, Isaac. *Guide to Prayer*. Ed. Harry Escott. London: Epworth Press, 1948.

PRAYER IN GENERAL

Barth, Karl. *Prayer*. Tr. Sara F. Terrien. Philadelphia: The Westminster Press, 1952.

Belden, Albert D. *The Practice of Prayer*. New York: Harper & Bros., 1954.

Bonnell, John S. *The Practice and Power of Prayer*. Philadelphia: The Westminster Press, 1954.

Buttrick, George A. *Prayer*. Nashville: Abingdon Press, 1942.

———. *So We Believe, So We Pray*. Nashville: Abingdon Press, 1951.

Casteel, John Laurence. *Rediscovering Prayer*. New York: Association Press, 1955.

Fleming, Daniel J. *The World at One in Prayer*. New York: Harper & Bros., 1942.

Harkness, Georgia. *Prayer and the Common Life*. Nashville: Abingdon Press, 1948.

Heiler, Friedrich. *Das Gebet*. 5 aufl. München: E. Reinhardt, 1923. The standard work. Not in print. Deserves a new translation.

———. *Prayer*. Ed. and tr. by Samuel McComb with the assistance of J. Edgar Park. New York: Oxford University Press, 1932. Omits able portions. Not in print.

Herman, Emily. *Creative Prayer*. New York: Harper & Bros., 1934.

Laubach, Frank. *Prayer, the Mightiest Force in the World*. Westwood, N.J.: Fleming H. Revell Co., 1946.

McFadyen, John E. *The Prayers of the Bible*. New York: A. C. Armstrong & Son, 1906. Not in print. Deserves reprinting.

Magee, John. *Reality and Prayer*. New York: Harper & Bros., 1957.

Stephens, John Underwood. *A Simple Guide to Prayer.* Nashville: Abingdon Press, 1957.

Stewart, George Shaw. *The Lower Levels of Prayer.* Nashville: Abingdon Press, 1939.

Wyon, Olive. *The School of Prayer.* 7th ed. London: Allenson & Co., Ltd., 1952. Paper.

PRIVATE PRAYER

Andrewes, Lancelot. *Private Devotions of Lancelot Andrewes.* Tr. John Henry Newman. Nashville: Abingdon Press, 1950.

Baillie, John. *A Diary of Private Prayer.* New York: Charles Scribner's Sons, 1949.

Day, Albert Edward. *An Autobiography of Prayer.* New York: Harper & Bros., 1952.

Fosdick, Harry Emerson. *The Meaning of Prayer.* New York: Association Press, 1915.

Fox, Selina F. (comp.). *A Chain of Prayer Across the Ages.* 7th ed. New York: E. P. Dutton & Co., Inc., 1943.

Gossip, Arthur J. *In the Secret Place of the Most High.* New York: Charles Scribner's Sons, 1947. Sermonic.

Kadel, William H. *Prayers for Every Need.* Richmond: John Knox Press, 1957.

Kosten, Andrew (ed.). *Devotions and Prayers of Martin Luther.* Grand Rapids: Baker Book House, 1956. Small.

Orchard, William E. *The Temple: A Book of Prayers.* New York: E. P. Dutton & Co., Inc., 1918.

Redpath, Alan. *Victorious Praying.* Westwood, N.J.: Fleming H. Revell Co., 1957. The Lord's Prayer.

Rees, Paul S. *Prayer and Life's Highest.* Grand Rapids: William B. Eerdmans Publishing Co., 1957.

Speer, Robert E. *Five Minutes a Day.* Philadelphia: The Westminster Press, 1943.

Stafford, Thomas A. *The Practice of His Presence.* Westwood, N.J.: Fleming H. Revell Co., 1940.

Tileston, Mary W. (ed.). *Prayers, Ancient and Modern.* New York: Grosset & Dunlap, 1928.

Trueblood, David Elton (ed.). *Dr. Johnson's Prayers.* New York: Harper & Bros., 1947.

Whyte, Alexander. *Lord, Teach Us to Pray.* London: Oliphants, Ltd., 1949. Sermons.

WORKS OF DEVOTION

Augustine. *Confessions.* Various editions.

Baillie, John. *A Diary of Readings.* New York: Charles Scribner's Sons, 1955.

Barrois, Georges A. *Pathways of the Inner Life.* Indianapolis: Bobbs-Merrill Co., Inc., 1956.

Baxter, Richard. *The Reformed Pastor.* Grand Rapids: Zondervan Publishing House, 1955.

————. *The Saints' Everlasting Rest.* Rev. ed. Grand Rapids: Zondervan Publishing House, 1957.

Bunyan, John. *The Pilgrim's Progress.* Various editions.

Fénelon, Francois. *Christian Perfection.* Ed. Charles F. Whitson. Tr. Mildred W. Stillman. New York: Harper & Bros., 1947.

Francis of Assisi. *Little Flowers.* Various editions.

Herbert, George. *The Country Parson.* London: S.C.M. Press, 1956.

Jones, E. Stanley. *Christian Maturity.* Nashville: Abingdon Press, 1957.

Kelly, Thomas A. *A Testament of Devotion.* New York: Harper & Bros., 1941.

Kempis, Thomas à. *Imitation of Christ.* Various editions.

Kepler, Thomas S. (ed.). *The Fellowship of the Saints.* Nashville: Abingdon Press, 1948. An anthology.

Kierkegaard, Sören. *Purity of Heart.* Tr. Douglas Van Steere. Rev. ed. New York: Harper & Bros., 1956.

Law, William. *A Serious Call to a Devout and Holy Life.* Ed. John Meister, et al. Philadelphia: The Westminster Press, 1948.

Luther, Martin. *Letters of Spiritual Counsel.* Ed. and tr. Theodore G. Tappert. Philadelphia: The Westminster Press, 1955.

Meyer, Frederick B. *Our Daily Walk.* Grand Rapids: Zondervan Publishing House, 1951.

Murray, Andrew. *With Christ in the School of Prayer.* Westwood, N.J.: Fleming H. Revell Co., 1956.

Oldham, J. H. *A Devotional Diary.* New York: Harper & Bros., 1931.

Palmer, W. Scott (ed.). *The Confessions of Jacob Boehme.* New York: Harper & Bros., 1954.

Pascal, Blaise. *Thoughts: An Apology for Christianity.* Ed. Thomas S. Kepler. Cleveland: The World Publishing Co., 1955.

Rutherford, Samuel. *Letters.* Ed. Frank E. Gaebelein. Chicago: Moody Press, 1951.

Sangster, W. E. *The Secret of Radiant Life.* Nashville: Abingdon Press, 1957.

Taylor, Jeremy. *Rule and Exercises of Holy Dying.* Ed. Thomas S. Kepler. Cleveland: The World Publishing Co., 1952.

———. *Rule and Exercises of Holy Living.* Ed. Thomas S. Kepler. Cleveland: The World Publishing Co., 1952.

Woolman, John. *Journal.* Ed. Janet Whitney. Chicago: Henry Regnery Co., 1951.

Youngdahl, Reuben K. N. *This Is God's Day.* Rock Island, Ill.: Augustana Book Concern, 1956. Radio daily devotions for the Church Year.

———

These lists of Related Readings aim to be representative, not exhaustive. They give the preference to works now in print, and by Protestants. The books represent various shades of belief, doctrinally. Even the ablest of such works must give way to Holy Scripture, as the supreme source of guidance for the leader in public prayer, always through the Holy Spirit. "When he, the Spirit of truth, is come, he will guide you into all truth." (John 16:13a.)

Index of
Persons and Subjects